KYLE'S B&B PRESENTS:

Drawings of Drew

OTHER BOOKS by GREG FOX

Kyle's Bed & Breakfast

Kyle's Bed & Breakfast: A Second Bowl of Serial

Kyle's Bed & Breakfast: Hot Off the Griddle

KYLE'S B&B PRESENTS:
Drawings of Drew

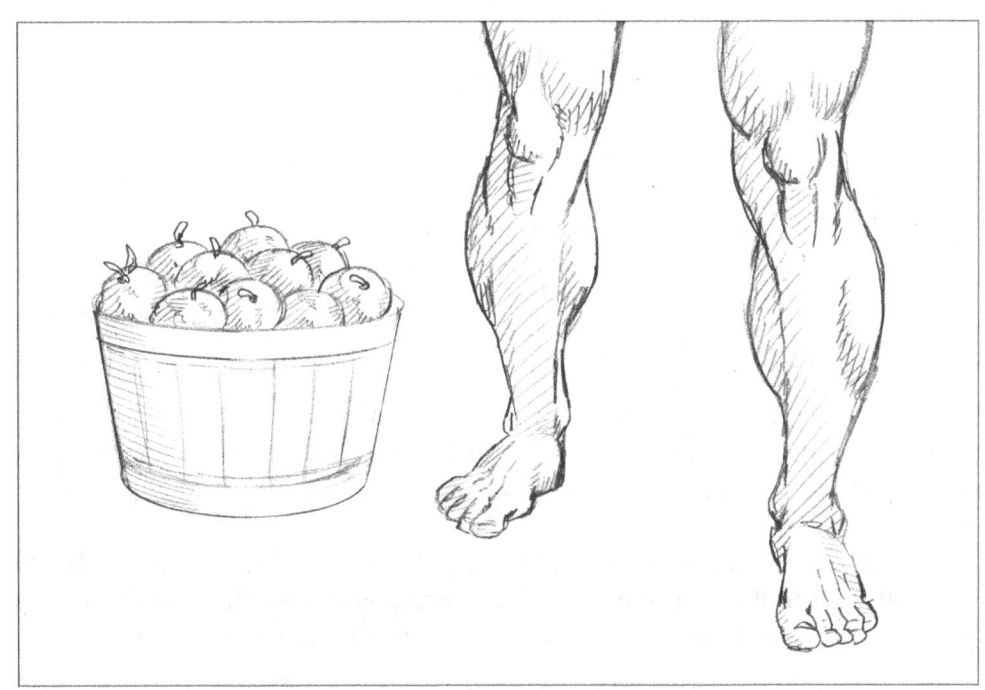

Greg Fox

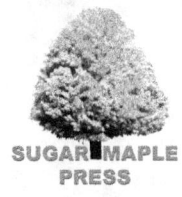

SUGAR MAPLE
PRESS

*For the readers of Kyle's B&B,
who continue to make this a most
extraordinary & blessed journey.*

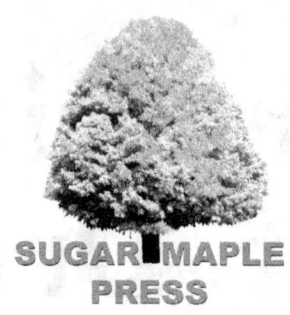

Sugar Maple Press

www.sugarmaplepress.com

e-mail: sugarmaplepress@yahoo.com

Sugar Maple Press edition: Copyright © 2014 by Greg Fox

All Sugar Maple Press titles are available at special quantity discounts for bulk purchases, for sales promotions, premiums, fundraising, educational or institutional use. Contact us at sugarmaplepress@yahoo.com for details.

ISBN-13:   978-0692215159
ISBN-10:   0692215158

First Sugar Maple Press Trade Paperback Printing: May, 2014

Table of Contents

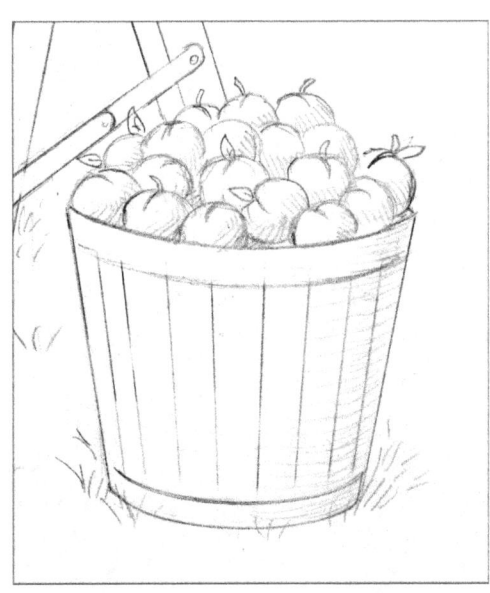

Kyle's B&B Presents: Drawings of Drew by Greg Fox

A Real Peach of a Guy...

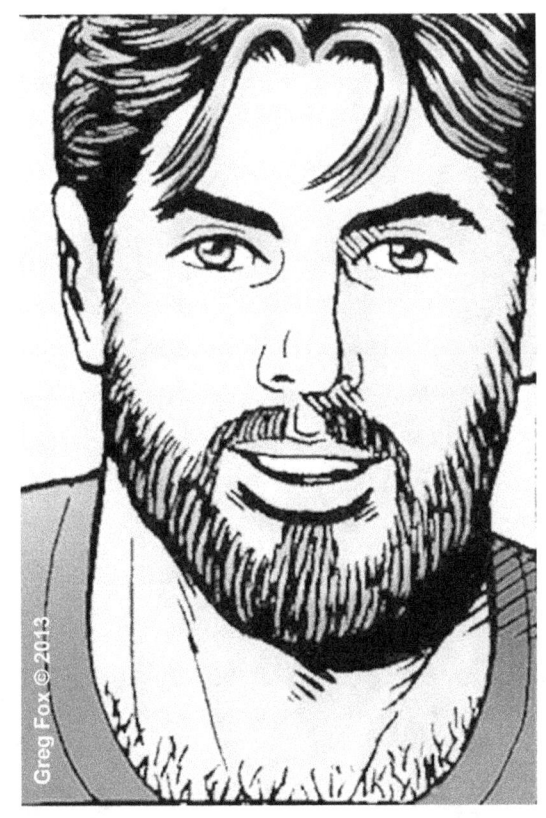

Greg Fox © 2013

Kyle's B&B Presents: Drawings of Drew by Greg Fox

There's just something about those southern guys.

One of the many delightful aspects of writing and drawing **Kyle's Bed & Breakfast** is when I get to introduce a new character into the comic strip. It's hard to predict how readers will react when a new face arrives at the B&B. Some quickly become beloved cast members, (like Jeff Olsen and Dave Yager). Others take a little more time, but eventually start to shine, (like Nick Ferrelli and the man who would ultimately capture Kyle's heart, Breyer Watkins). There are rare gems like Price Kingsbury, who become the type of machiavellian character that readers "love to hate". And then there are several characters who most readers would've preferred I'd posted a "no vacancies" sign on the door when they showed up on the steps of the B&B, (they shall remain nameless, although a certain French guy comes to mind...).

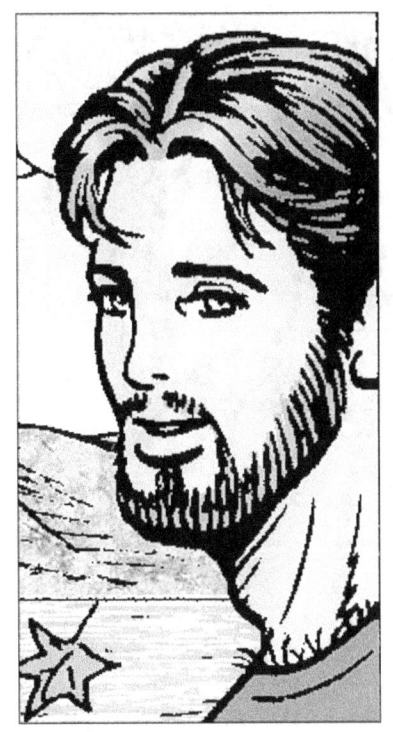

Drew Danvers was a hit right out of the gate. He was initially brought in as a potential love interest/sparring partner for Lance Powers in episode # 343, (October, 2012). Now if you're at all familiar with **Kyle's B&B**, you'll know that Lance's love affairs are notoriously short-lived. He's built a significant reputation as a "player", and we'd seen him have fiery-yet-brief dalliances with a housemate, Eduardo Alvarez, (ended badly) ...a short-term houseguest, Jean-Pierre Chevignon, (ended even *worse*) ...a client, Max Edgington, (ended *horrifically*) ...and a

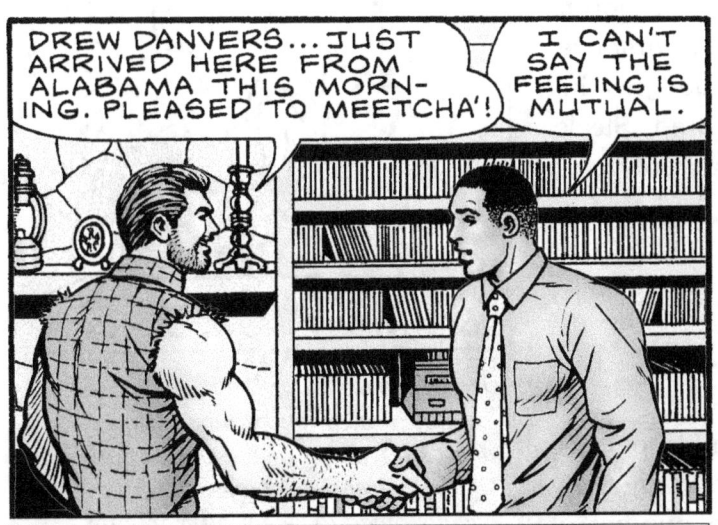

Above: Episode # 343 - Drew arrives and meets Lance. Friction from the very beginning!

number of one-night "tricks" in between. His most substantial relationship to date had been with Sean O'Grady, an Irish priest-in-training. And while that particular liaison did reveal a somewhat softer side of Lance, the relationship itself was, by its very nature, doomed to failure.

And then Drew showed up. A cocky, slightly abrasive Alabama country boy... probably the last person Lance would be drawn to. But, as is so often the case, opposites attract, and before long, serious sparks were flying between these two.

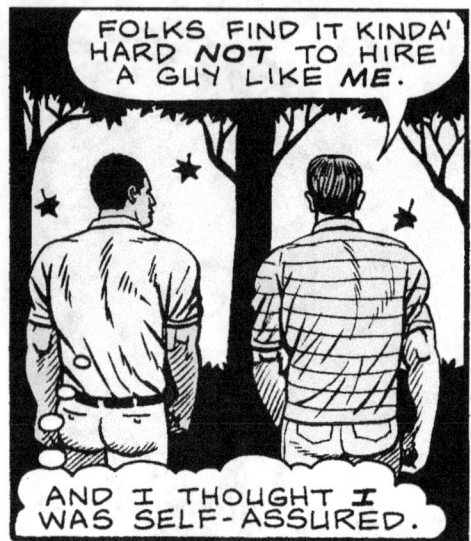

Lance & Drew on their first date. Drew's cockiness may have put off Lance a bit, at first...but it only seemed to endear him to readers. (Episode # 344)

And Lance wasn't the only one falling for Drew. Within days of his first appearance, readers responded with an unusually large amount of e-mails, blog comments, and Facebook messages... asking me to show more of him, and to *please* not let this be another one of Lance's throw-away tricks.

Soon after this I was in Los Angeles for Bent-Con, an LGBT-oriented comics convention, where I had the privilege to meet in person a whole lot of wonderful, enthusiastic **Kyle's B&B** readers. And pretty amazingly, almost every one of them asked me about Drew, and wanted me to *promise* I wasn't going to send him packing like all of Lance's other conquests, (poor Lance. He's developed quite a reputation over the years!).

Well the truth was... I had no plans to "send him packing", as I was having too much fun writing and drawing

him! Although I couldn't promise that he and Lance would have a smooth road in their relationship, (and they didn't; in fact, that road was pretty much the definition of "rocky"), I *did* want to keep his cowboy boots around the B&B as long as possible.

The readers spoke decisively just a couple of months later, when Drew Danvers topped the first-ever **Kyle's B&B** "Man of the Year" readers poll, beating out long-time reader favorites like Brad Steele. Rather astounding, considering Drew had only been in the strip for 3 months at that point. (And he'd go on to repeat that win in 2013, too! Winning with a hefty 44% of the vote, his closest competition, again, being Brad, a distant second-place with 10% of the vote).

What was it about Drew that was winning over so many readers? Yes, it's obvious he's a ruggedly handsome man. But there have been a number of handsome men in the comic strip over the years who hadn't generated anywhere *near* the level of interest that Drew had.

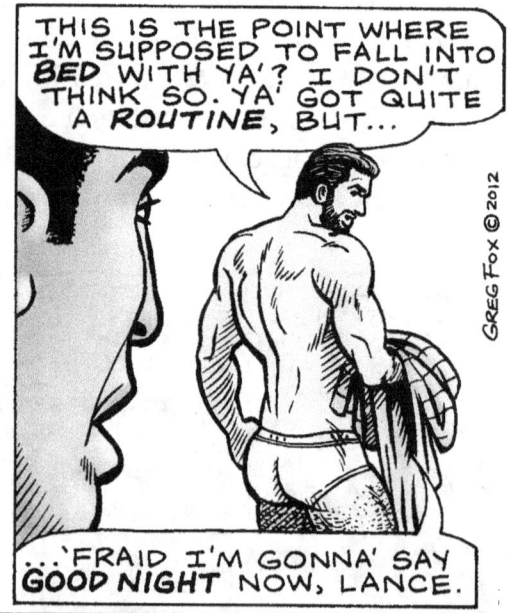

Drew surprised a lot of readers, and Lance, too, when he turned down Lance's advances at the conclusion of their first date. Lance wasn't accustomed to rejection from any man, which perhaps fueled his interest in Drew even more. (Episode # 345)

The impression I get from readers, overall, is this: they see Drew as a *good man*. A guy who's not afraid to speak his mind, to get his hands dirty, and to do the right thing. A "stand up guy".

For example, when he went out of his way to help Rudy, (the B&B's first senior citizen resident). Rudy was facing the prospect of being sent off the live in an elder-care facility by his well-meaning but somewhat clueless family. He was, understandably, frightened and confused by the prospect. Yet Drew stepped in, helping to calm Rudy's fears by taking him to visit and inspect the facility for himself ...and also assuring Rudy that he'd be looking out for him, and would come and rescue him if for *any* reason he felt uncomfortable there. (And then taking Rudy out for pizza afterwards!).

It seems that this concern for others' welfare is an essential part of who Drew *is*. He works as a licensed social worker, and always seems ready to help out anyone in need.

He even seems to have developed somewhat of a tenuous friendship with Price Kingsbury, the B&B's other resident southern boy, (who, unlike Drew, has never

*Kentucky boy Price Kingsbury trying to ingratiate himself with fellow southerner Drew. Kyle's B&B readers were suspicious about Price's motives. And in this case... they were **right** to be suspicious!. (Episode # 382)*

Lance & Drew's first kiss threw Lance off balance, (in more ways than one!). Up to this point, Lance was having serious doubts about having any sort of involvement with Drew. However, Drew, was not to be so easily written off! But it would still take a bit more time for Lance to truly warm up to Drew, despite this obviously cataclysmic kiss! (Episode # 346)

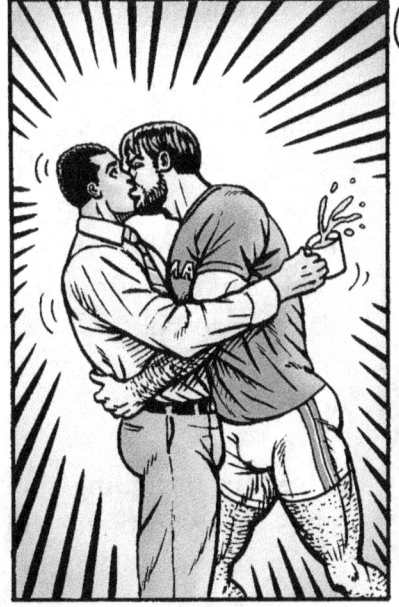

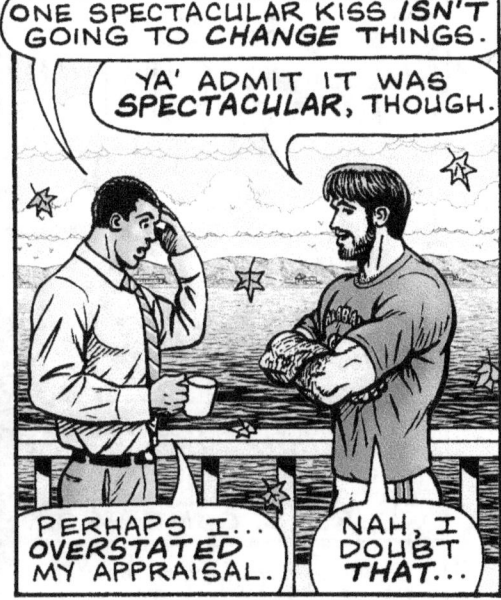

been in any danger of winning the B&B's "Man of the Year" contest).

In any case, as popular as Drew was becoming amongst readers, I hadn't planned on releasing a *book* devoted solely to *him*. So, how exactly did this book come about?

First of all...

SPOILER ALERT

(If you haven't already read the "Is Drew a Male Prostitute" storyline, you may want to skip over this part!)

Part of Drew's backstory is that his family in Alabama owns a peach orchard, and a big part of his life was spent working the orchard, picking peaches. The "Dixie Peach" tattoo on his backside was his way of commemorating that.

That tattoo would lead to trouble. Floyd Nelson, a business rival of Lance's, recognized Drew at an awards dinner he'd accompanied Lance to, and claimed that Drew was a male prostitute he'd hired at one time for sex. Lance initially balked at this, until Nelson offered up proof: he knew about Drew's hidden "Dixie Peach" tattoo.

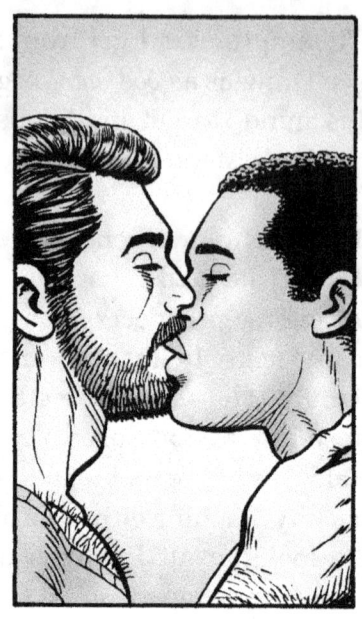

*It took a little while for some of their initial misunderstandings to get resolved. But once they were, Drew & Lance finally had their first **real** kiss. And if was well worth the wait! (Episode # 350)*

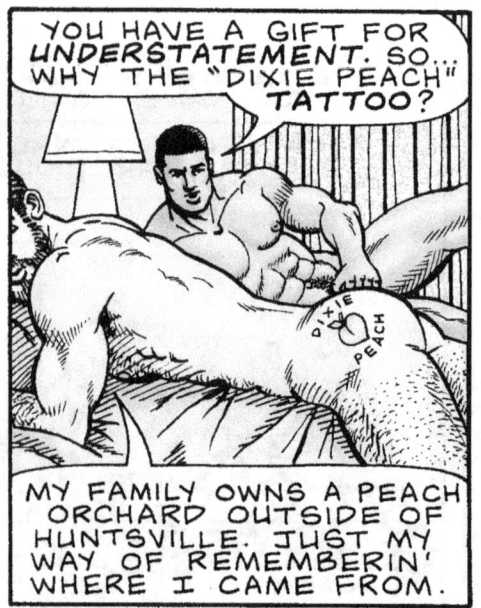

YOU HAVE A GIFT FOR UNDERSTATEMENT. SO... WHY THE "DIXIE PEACH" TATTOO?

DIXIE PEACH

MY FAMILY OWNS A PEACH ORCHARD OUTSIDE OF HUNTSVILLE. JUST MY WAY OF REMEMBERIN' WHERE I CAME FROM.

Drew explains the origins of that notorious tattoo. (Episode # 350)

As it would turn out, Drew *wasn't* a male prostitute. Nelson had seen nude pictures of Drew from a poetry book he'd posed for while in college, and seized that information about Drew's tattoo to mess with Lance, (which, of course, led to more drama and misunderstandings at the B&B. Ah, the fun never ends!).

Immediately after this storyline ran, I started receiving a new set of inquiries from **Kyle's B&B** readers. Was I planning to publish an *actual* book of poetry featuring nude pictures of Drew? And if not... would I consider doing it?

It was an intriguing prospect. I do a fair amount of "classical style" figure drawing on the side, something that goes back to my college days of figure drawing classes. (I know, some folks call it "life drawing", but in

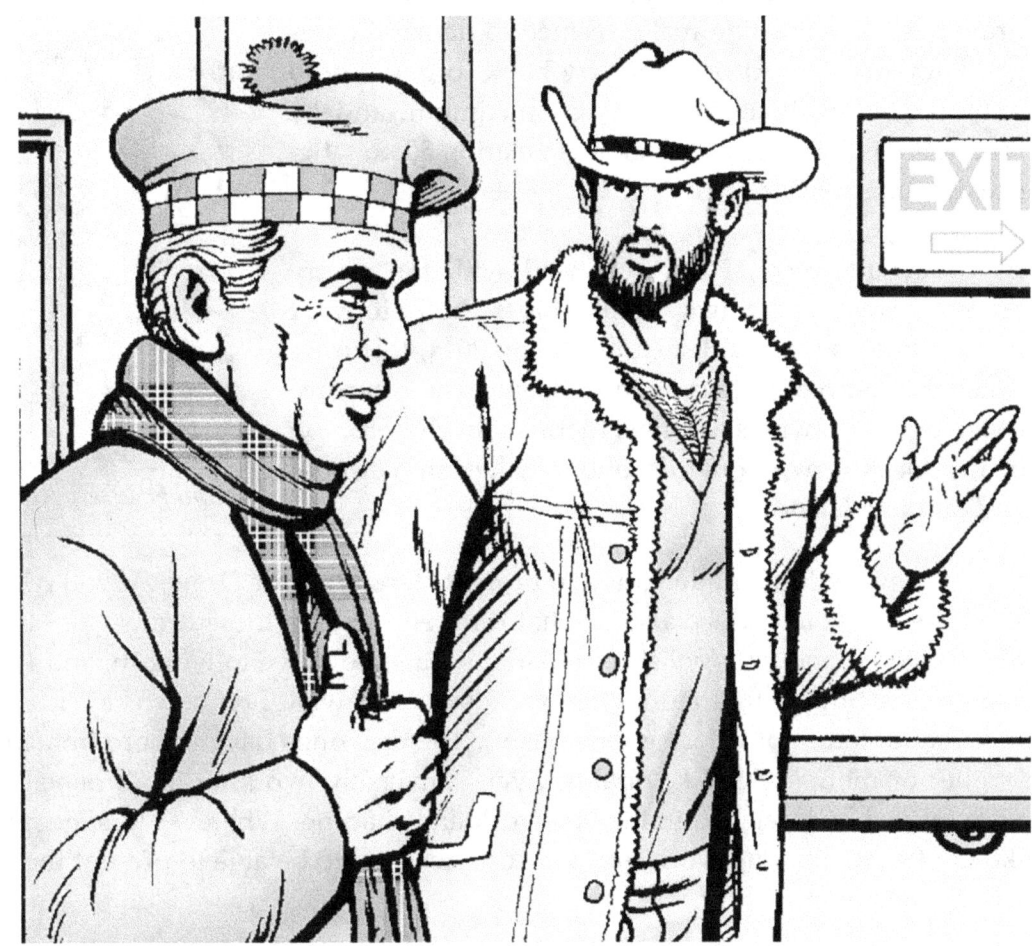

my experience, it's always been figure drawing. But I digress...). These days, with the comic strip keeping me quite busy drawing, I don't get to go to as many figure drawing groups as I'd like to, but I do try to go at least once a month to any of several different figure drawing groups here in the New York metro area, and I also occasionally get hired to do individual or couples' portraits.

The idea of doing a bunch of figure drawings of the Drew Danvers character, and putting them together into some sort of a poetry anthology seemed like a fun idea. I wouldn't claim to be any kind of an expert on poetry, but I did have some college experience with it, and was happy to find that there's a wealth of great classical poetry out there that's just waiting to be published. I even found a theme rather quickly: nature poetry, (it seemed like a good match for drawings of Draw that would be, ahem... *au naturel*).

About halfway through the project, though, I realized that the drawings would be better suited to stand on their own. The poetry book was going to be published in a smaller format, (6" x 9"), and these new drawings I was creating really seemed to demand a larger, "pin-up" size. Also, the poetry book format would only allow for about 20 drawings maximum, and by that point, I'd, (crazily), set a goal of creating 50 new figure drawings of Drew.

(If you're interested, I did go ahead with the poetry book anyway. **The Sugar Maple Press Anthology of Nature Poems** was published in March, 2014, featuring a stellar line-up of classical nature poems, and, in place of the figure drawings of Drew, there's a lovely selection of my black & white nature photos taken in Vermont and on Long Island).

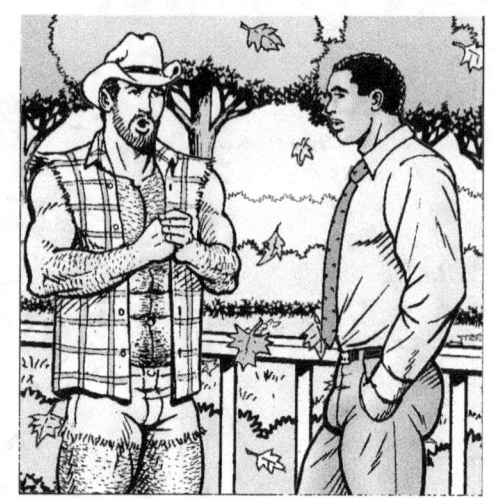

Another lovely Autumn day at the B&B!

And so, now, at last, I'm delighted to present **"Drawings of Drew"**. If you're familiar with my comics work, you'll notice a somewhat different style in these drawings. My comics work is inked, colored and very polished looking; it's a style I love to work in, and I'm not looking to change that. But my figure drawing work is done in what I refer to as a "classical style". It's all pencil, no inking, (or coloring, obviously). The drawings have a more immediate, sometimes rougher or more sketch-like quality... yet, conversely, working in all pencil allows me to be more refined and detailed in the line work and shading. Whatever it is, people seem to really like my figure drawing work, and I'm super-excited to be able to present these new drawings here in one volume!

I purposely made the **Drawings** section of this book single-paged, (meaning, each drawing has a blank page behind it. So that if you want to matte and/or frame any of these drawings,

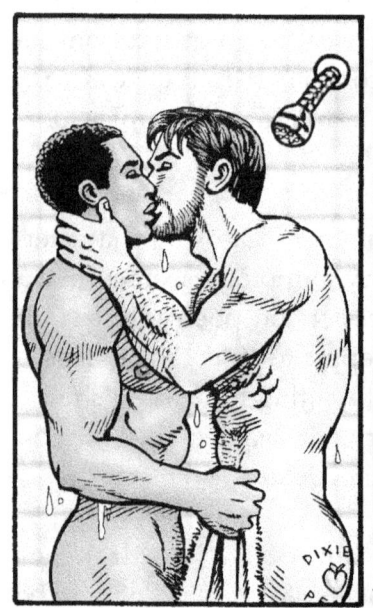

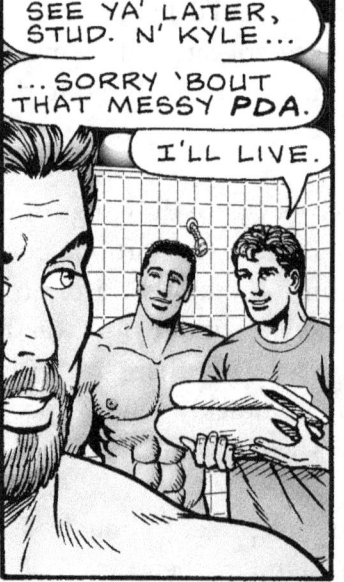

you don't need to choose between two drawings on either side of a page). There are also page-removal and framing suggestions on page 126, if you're so inclined. And all the drawings are purposely sized to fit into a standard 8" x 10" frame. (Also see page 126 for info about sending me pics of your hanged drawings of Drew!).

But for now, enough with the talking. Let's get to the drawings, shall we?

The Drawings

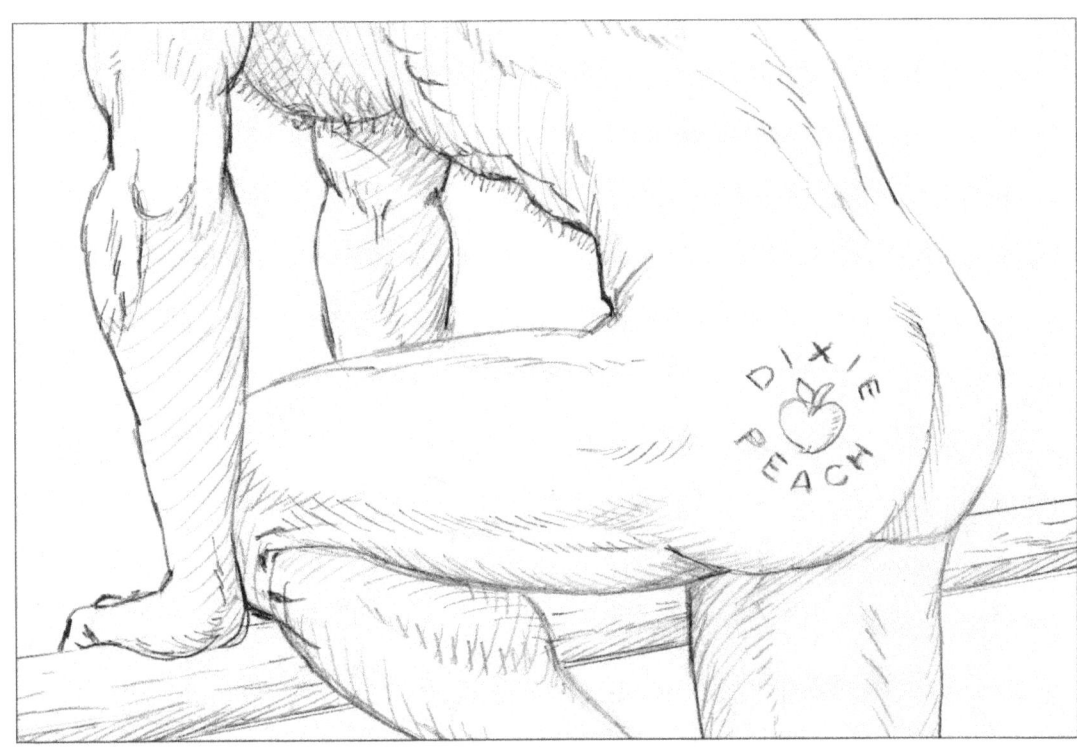

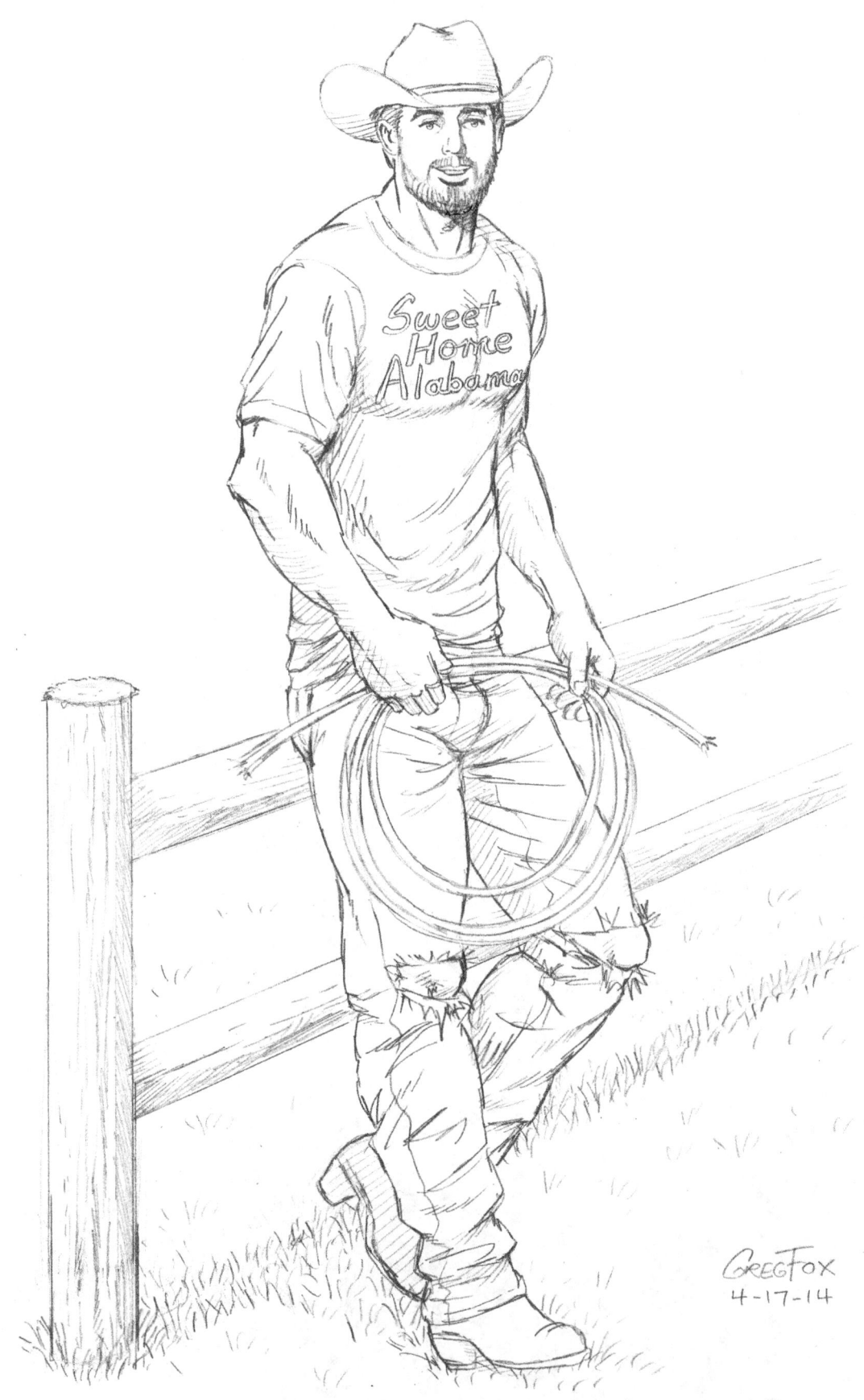

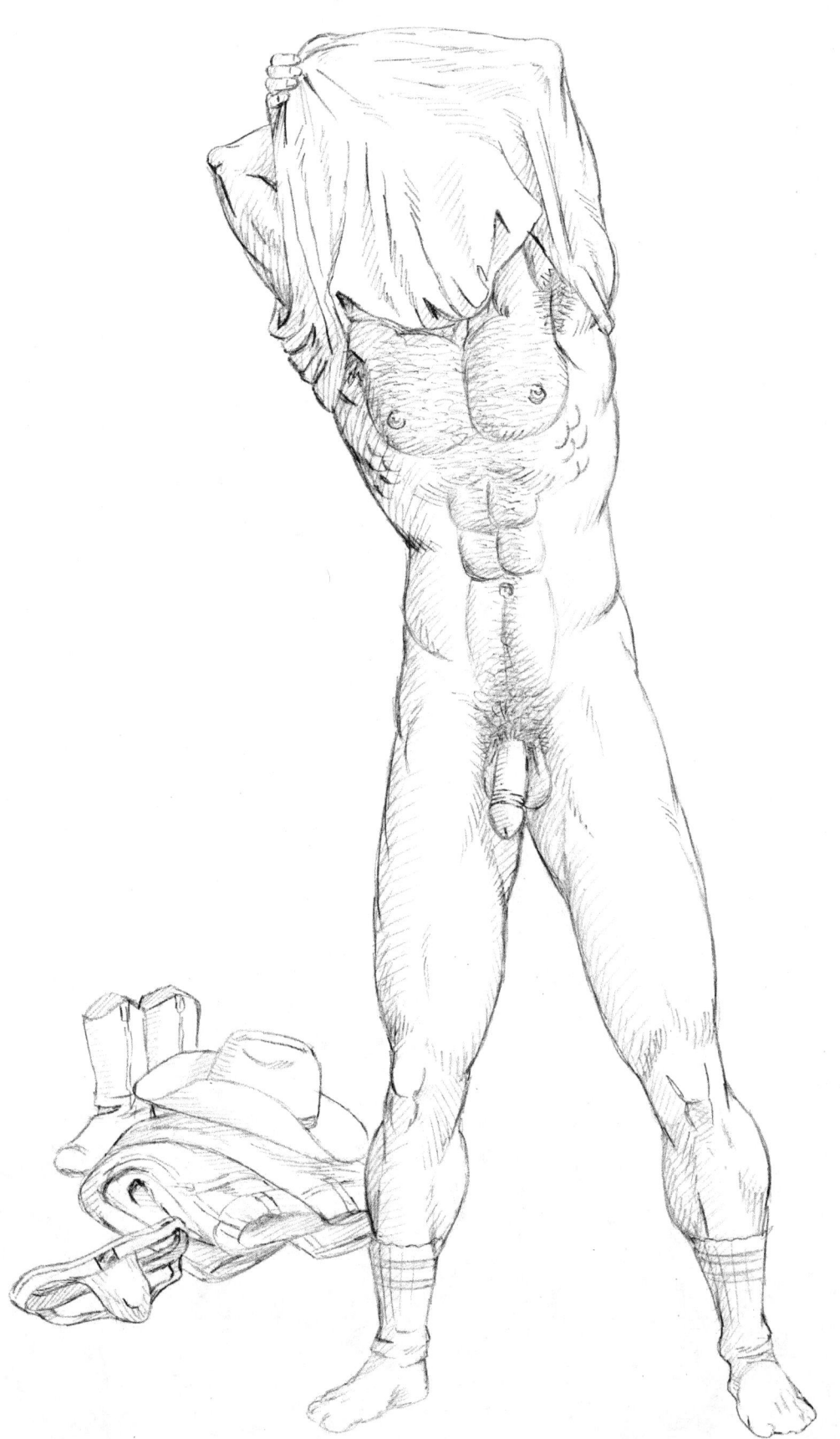

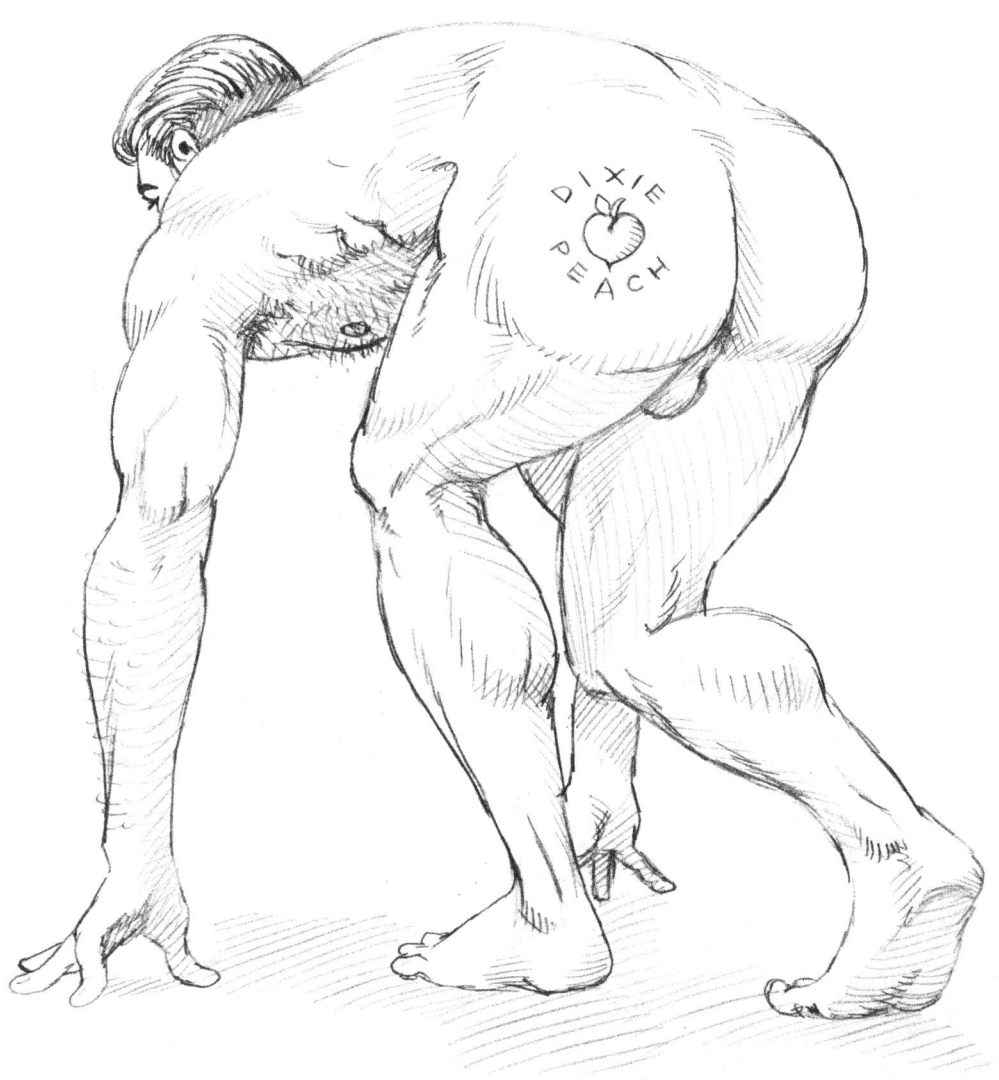

GregFox
2-26-14

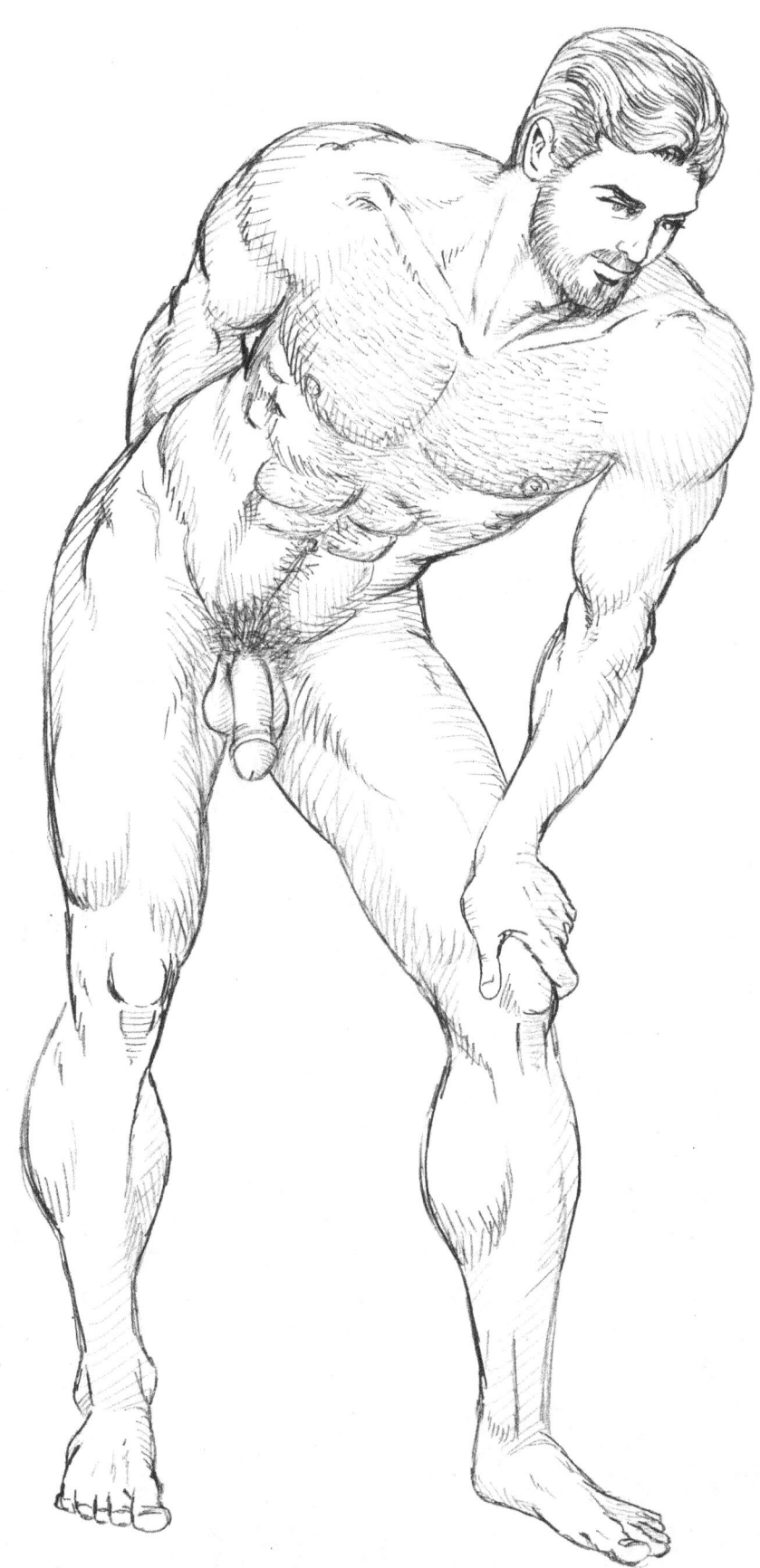

GregFox
4-1-14

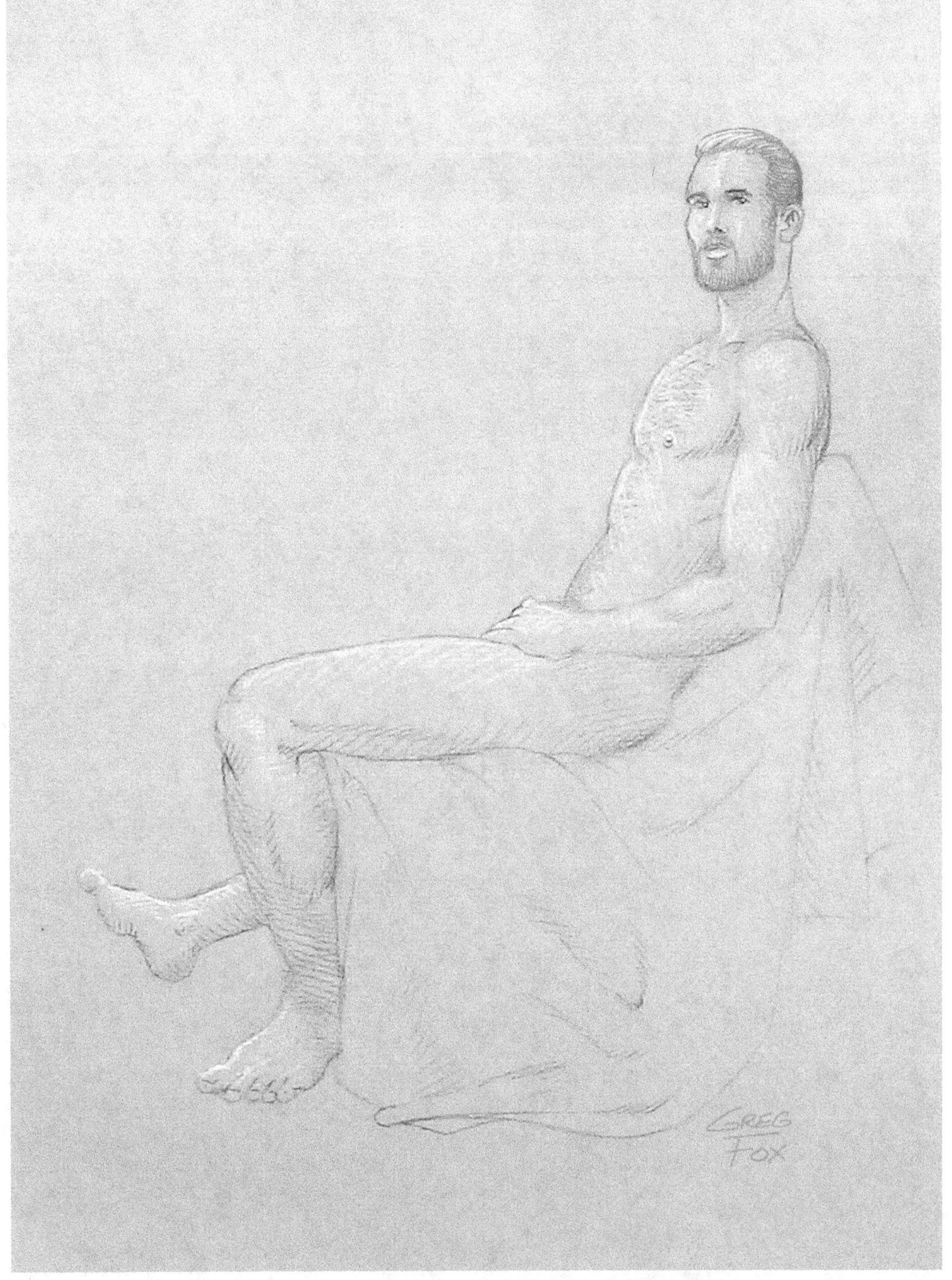

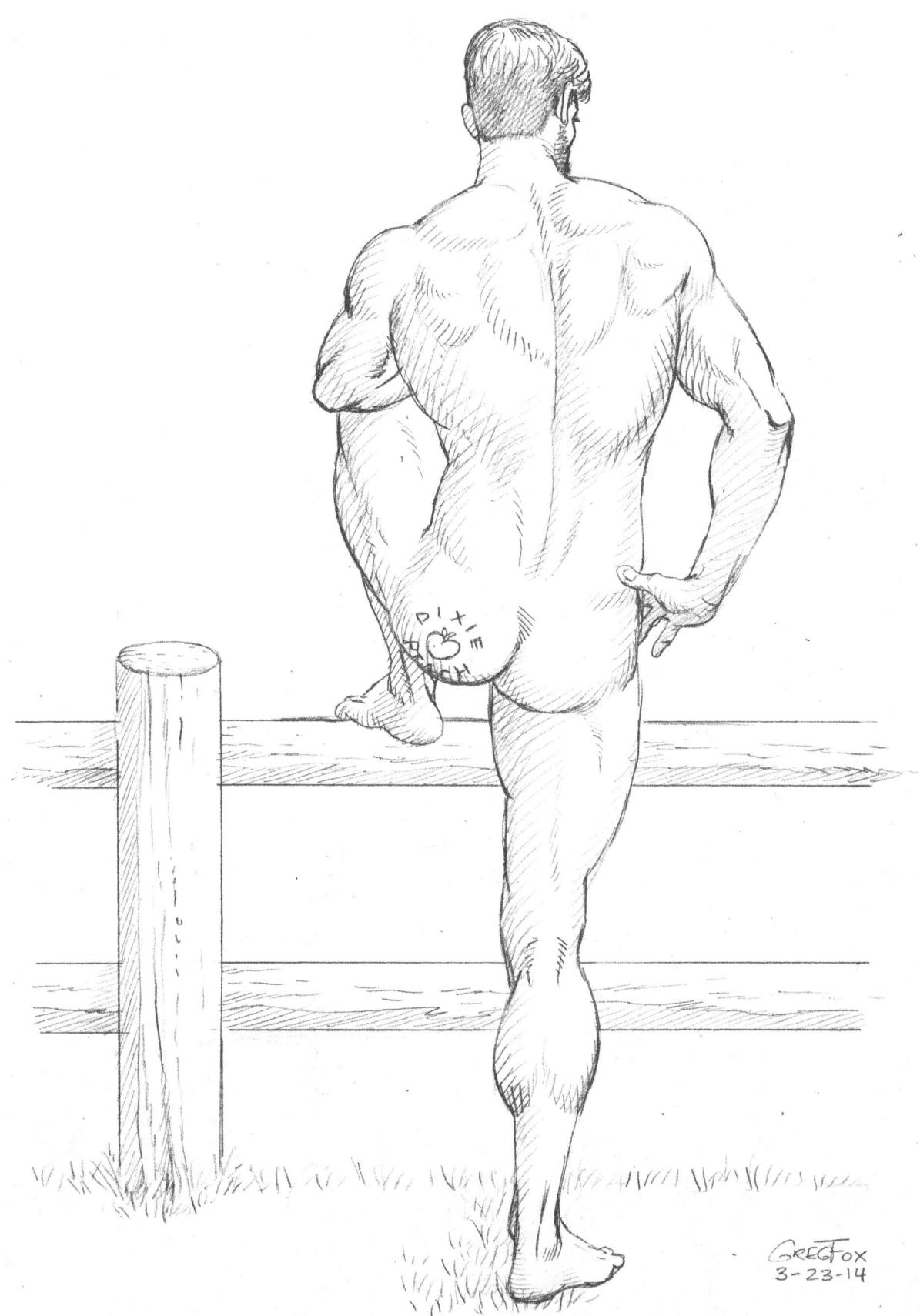

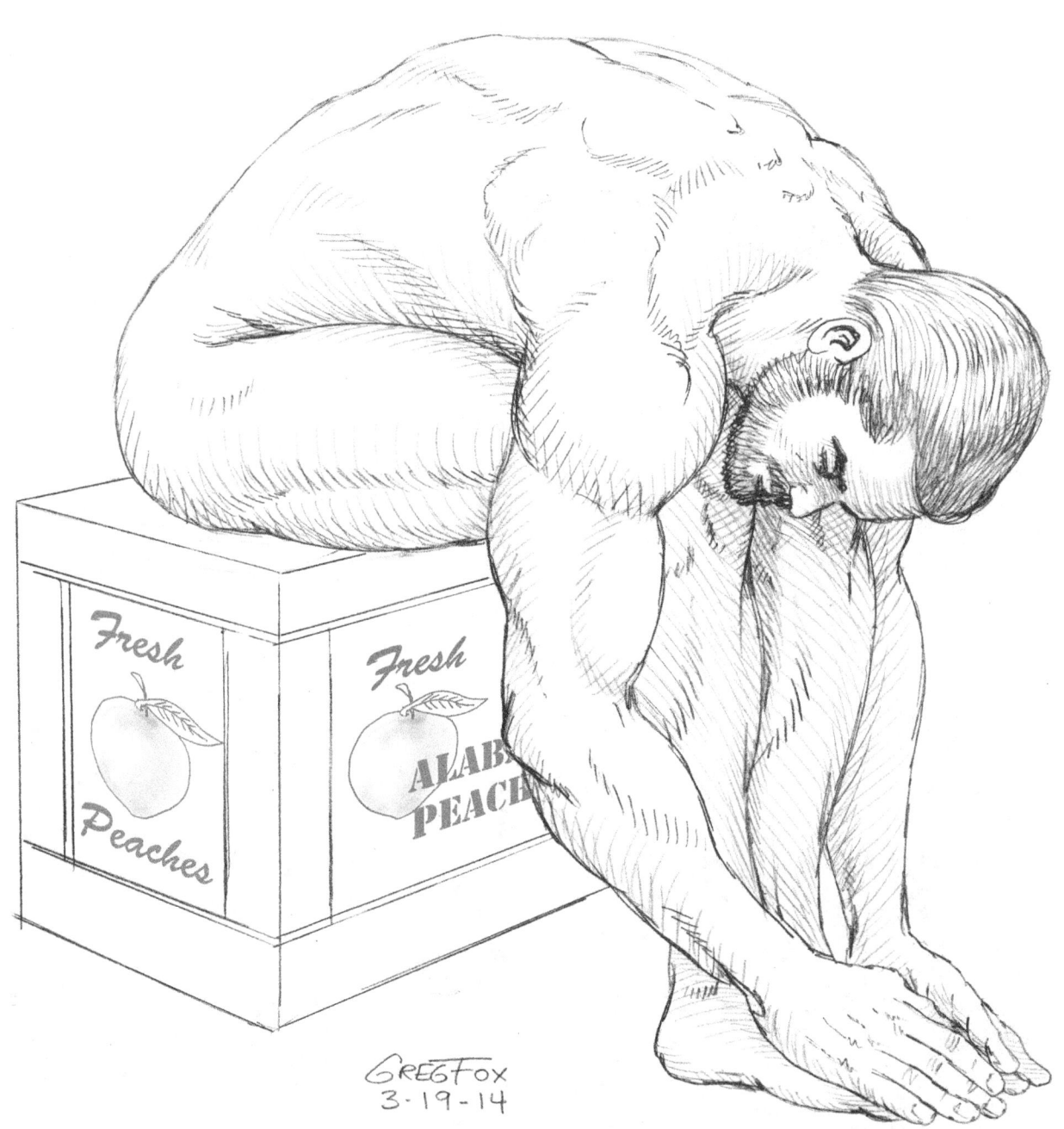

Fresh
Peaches

Fresh
ALAB
PEACH

GregFox
3-19-14

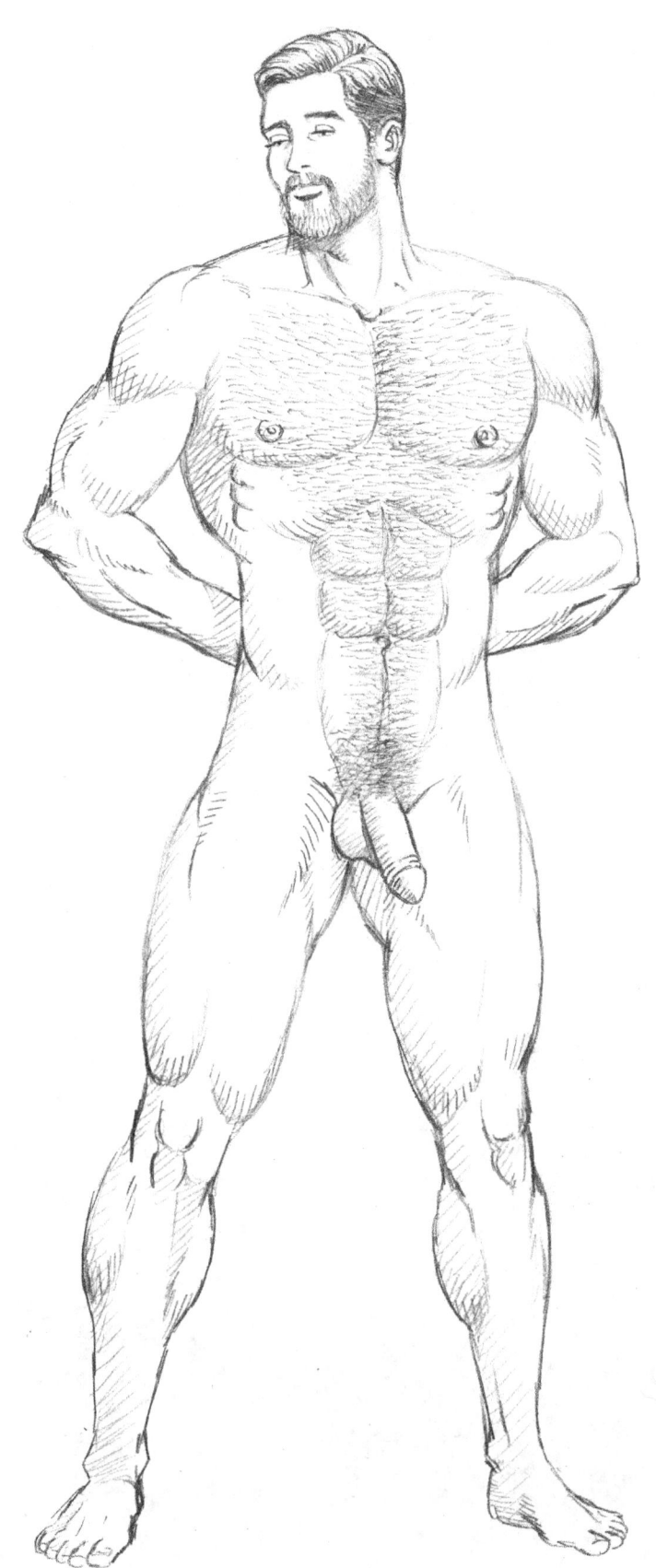

GregFox
3-9-14

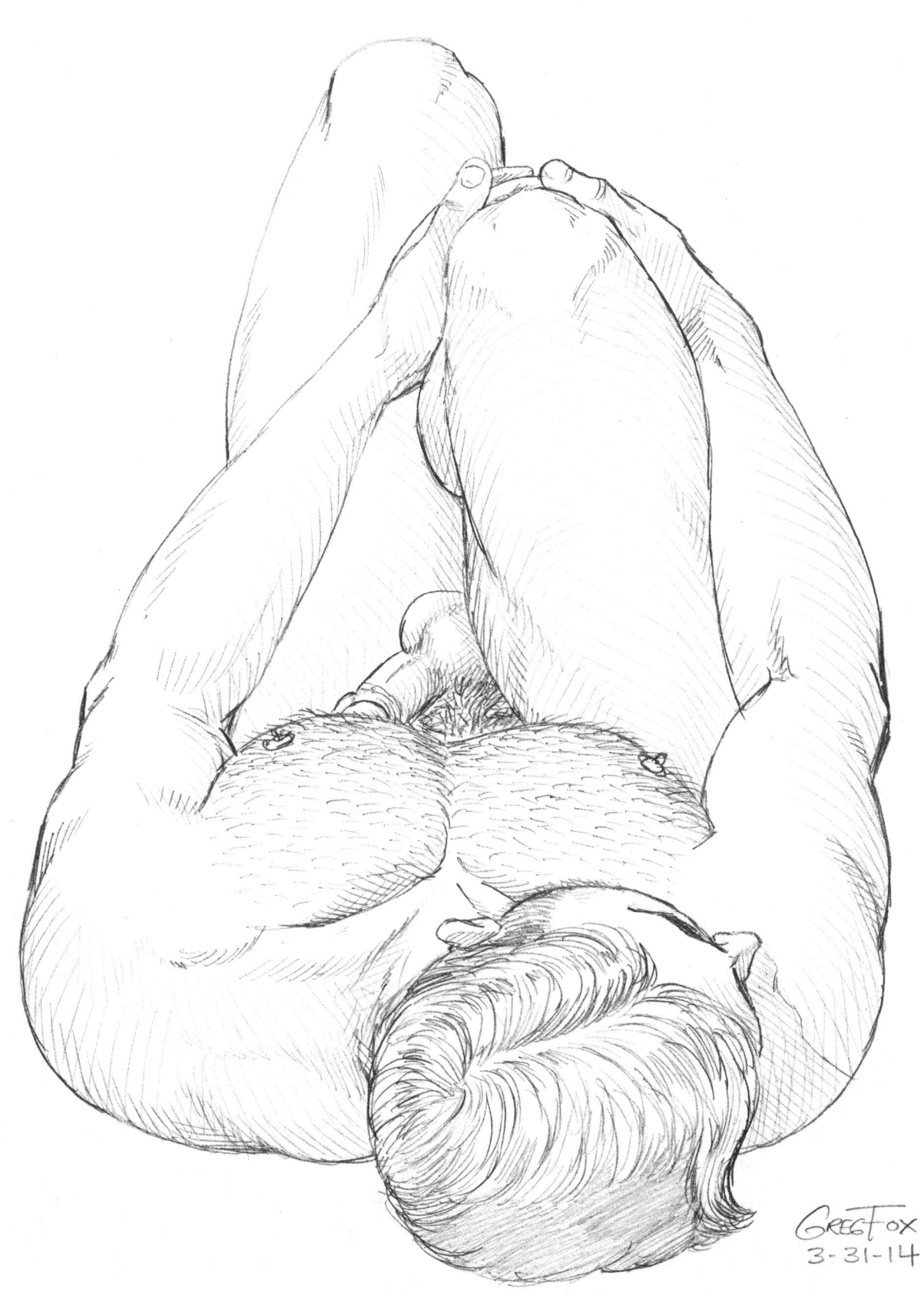

GregFox
3-31-14

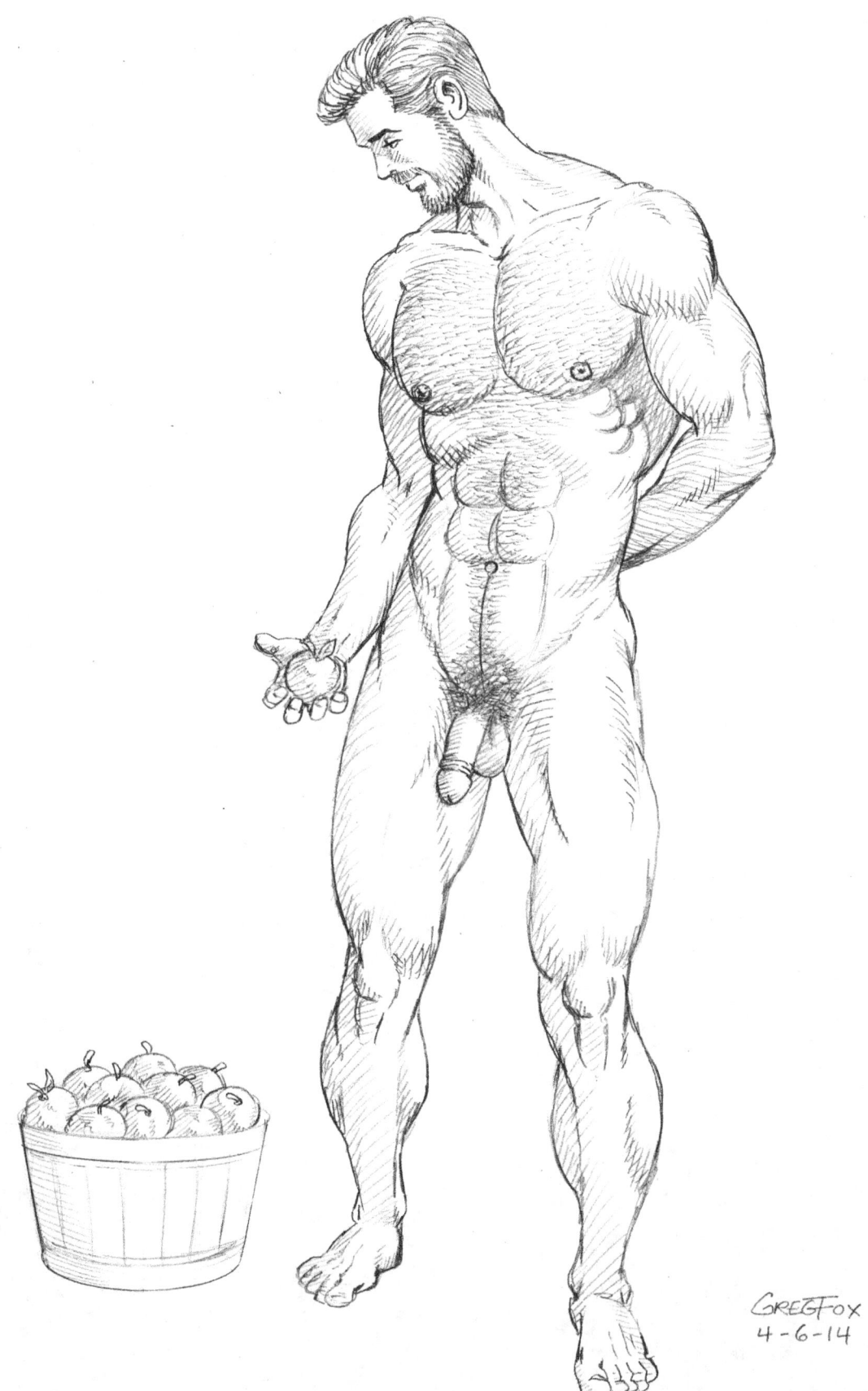

GregFox
4-6-14

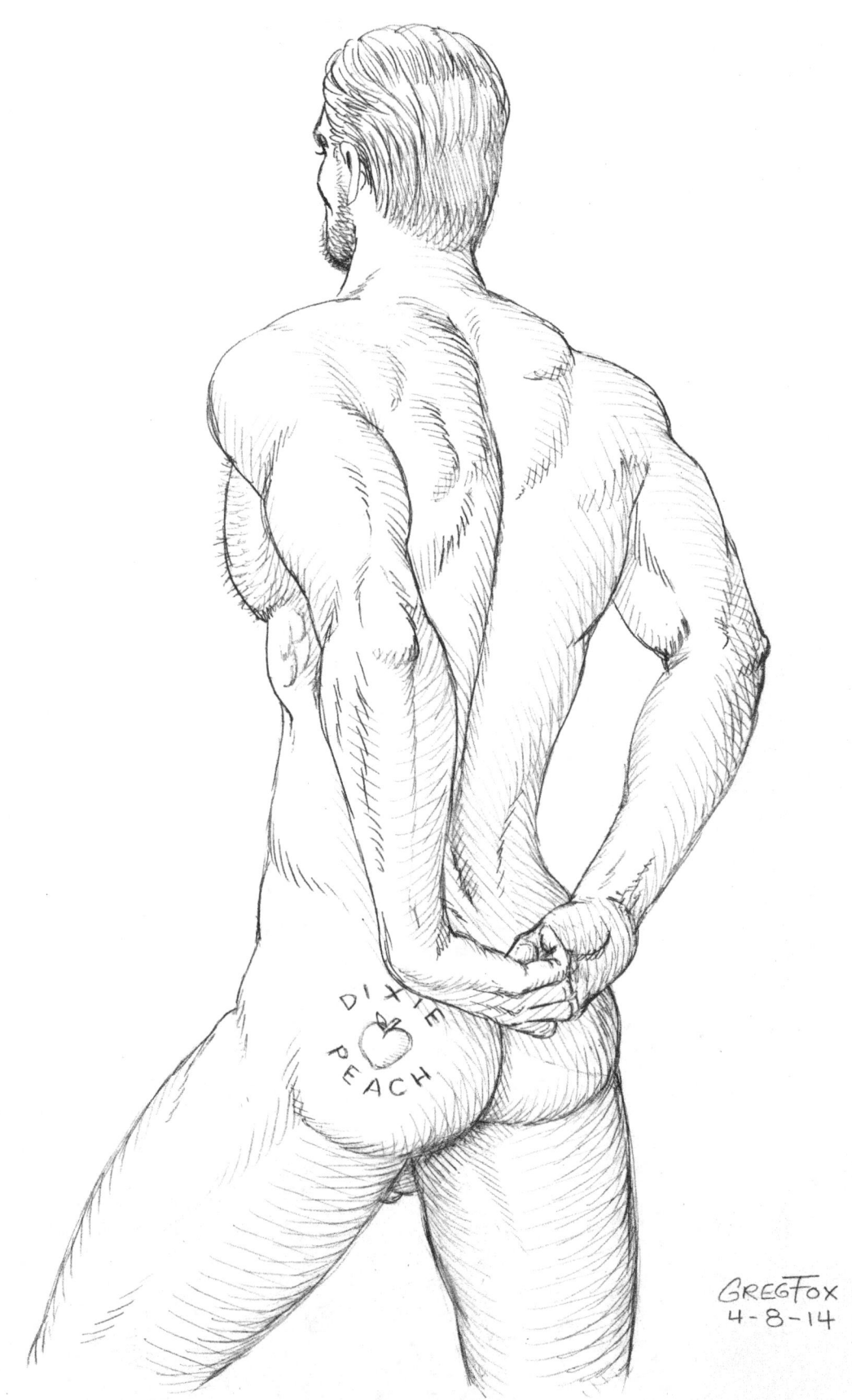

GregFox
4-8-14

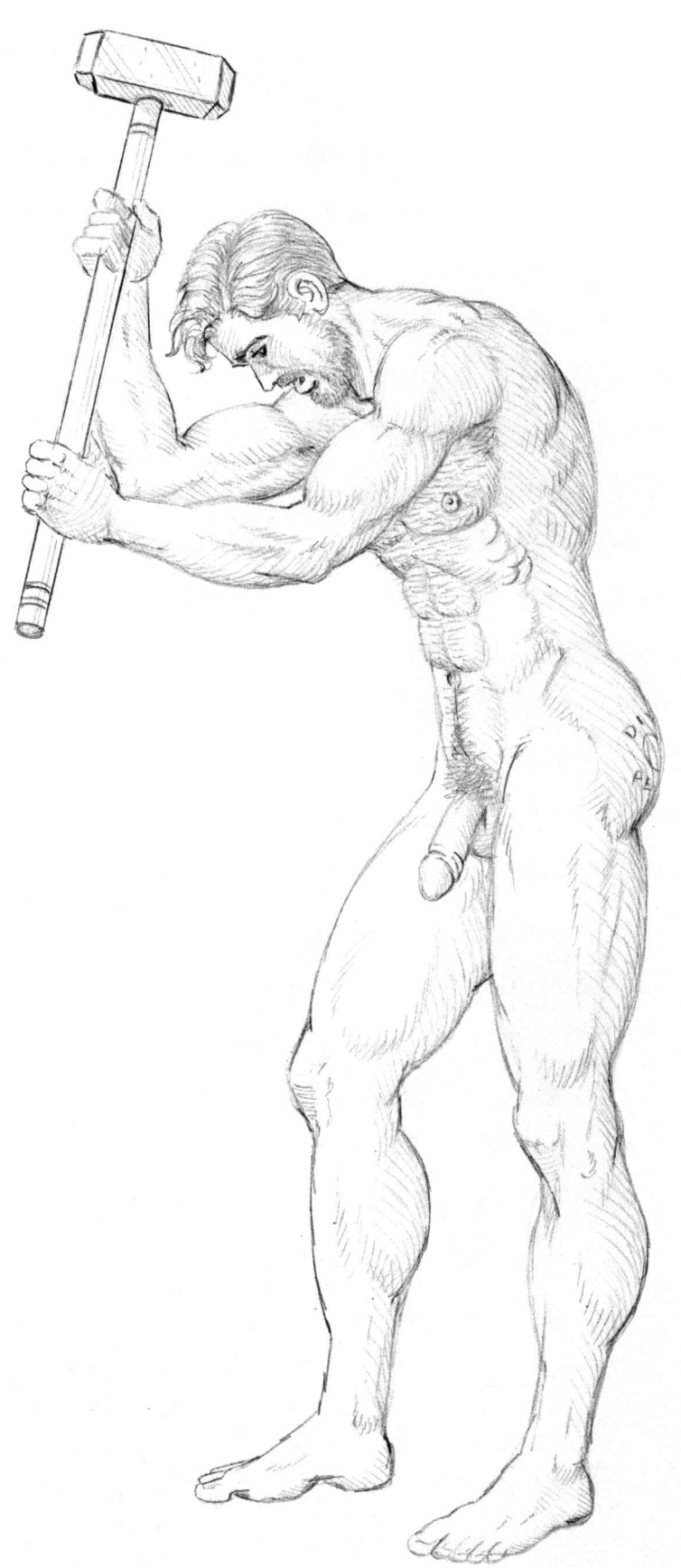

GregFox
4-20-14
EASTER

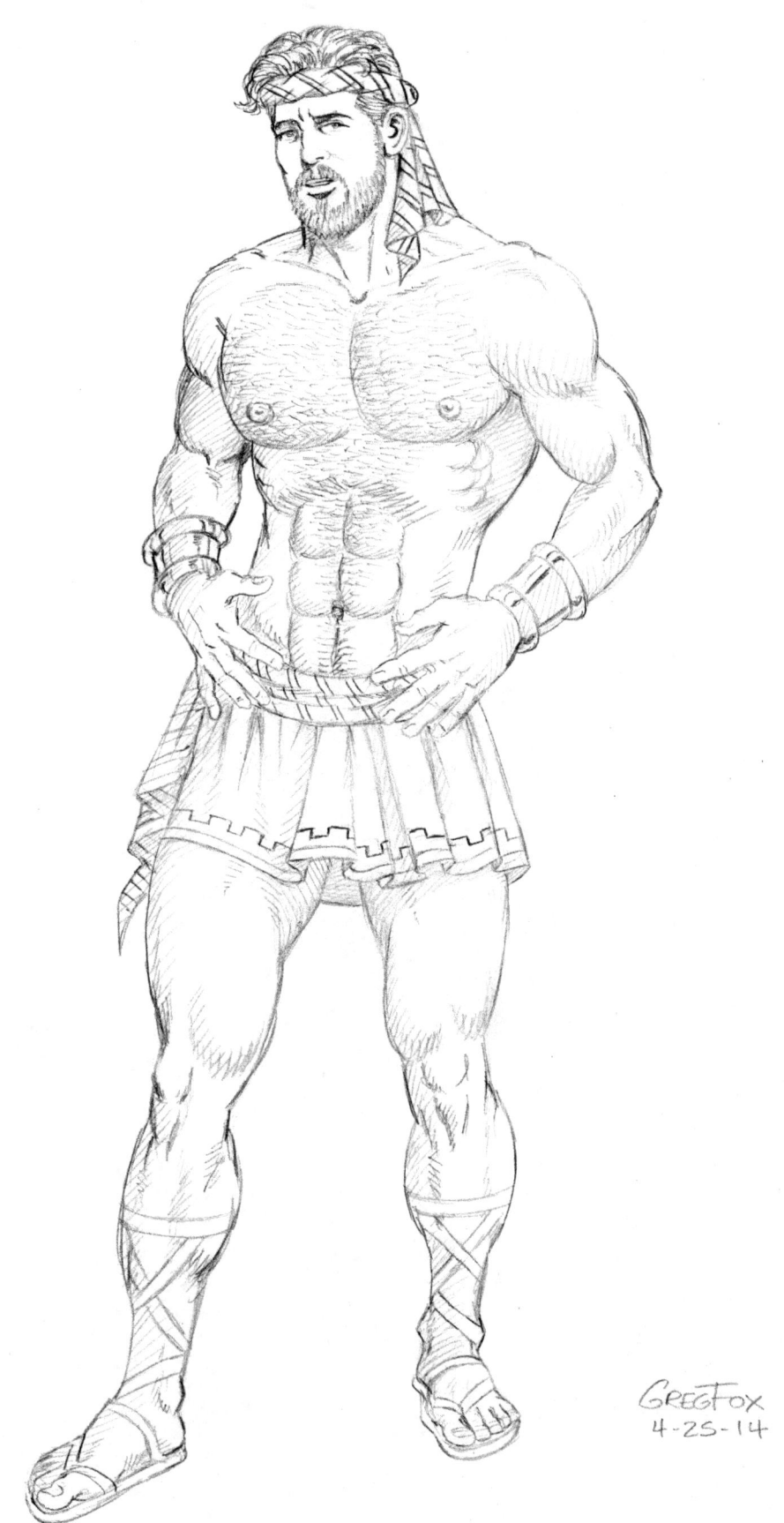

GregFox
4-25-14

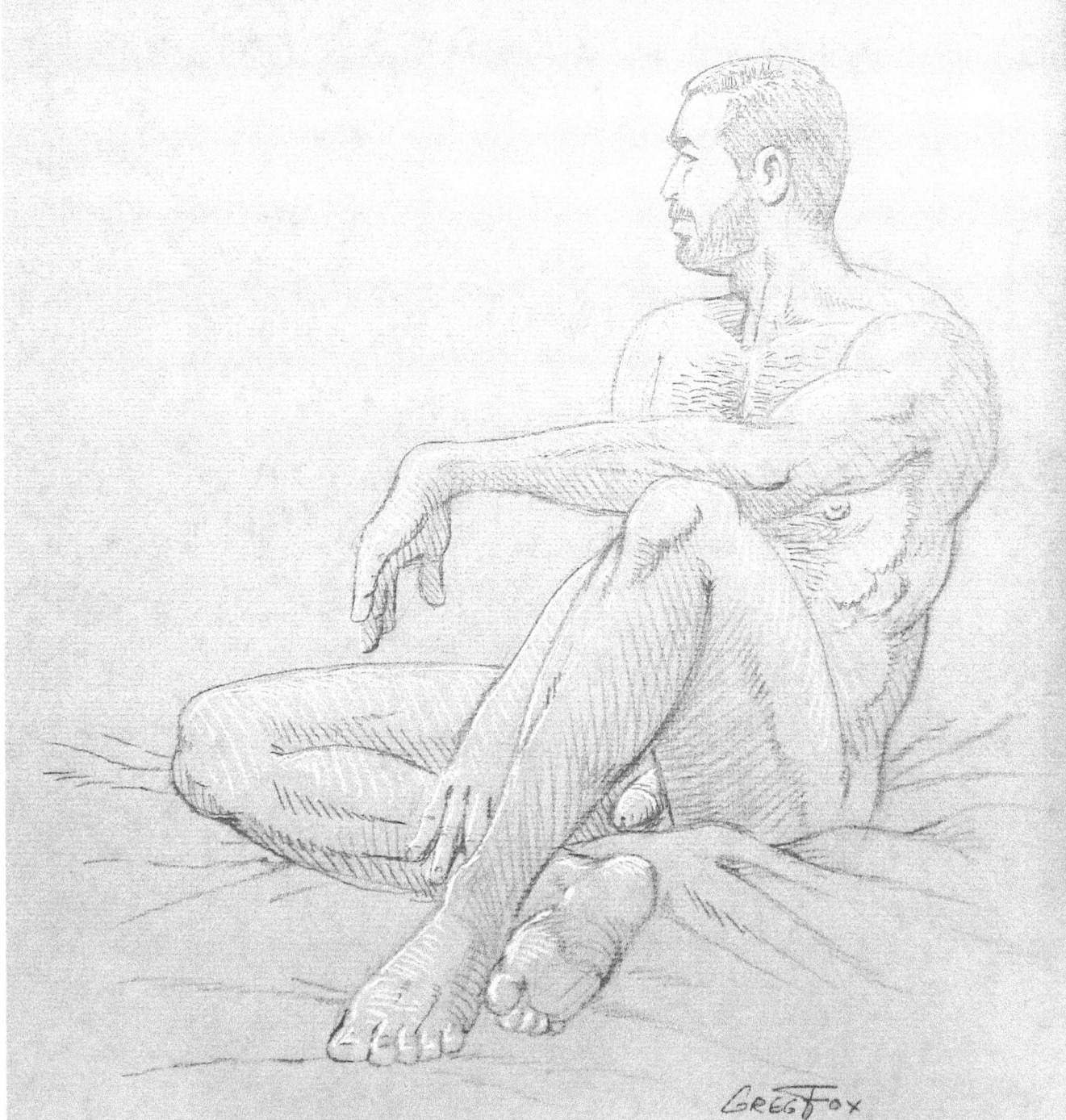

GregFox
2-28-09

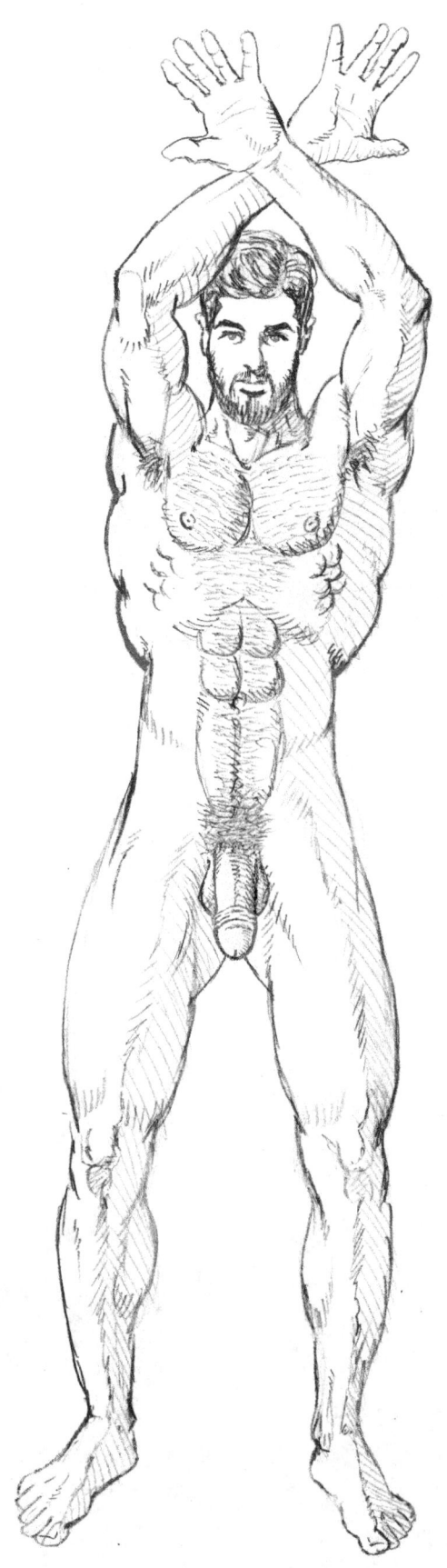

GregFox
3-6-14

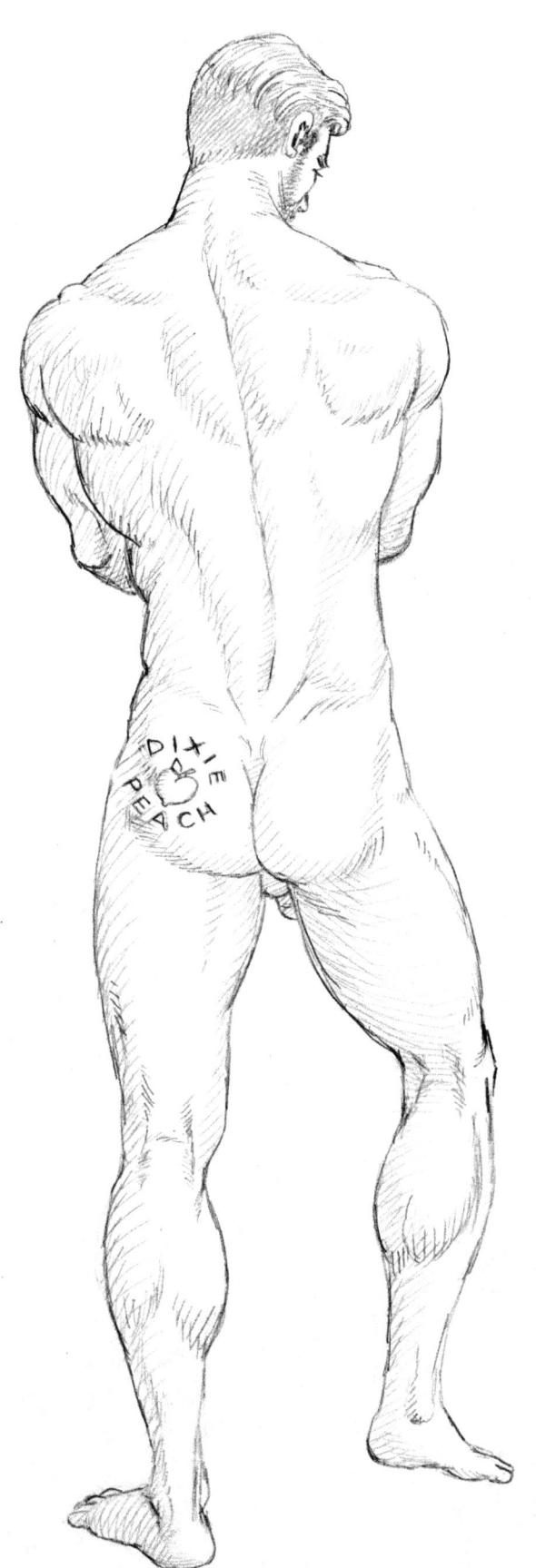

GregFox
4-5-14

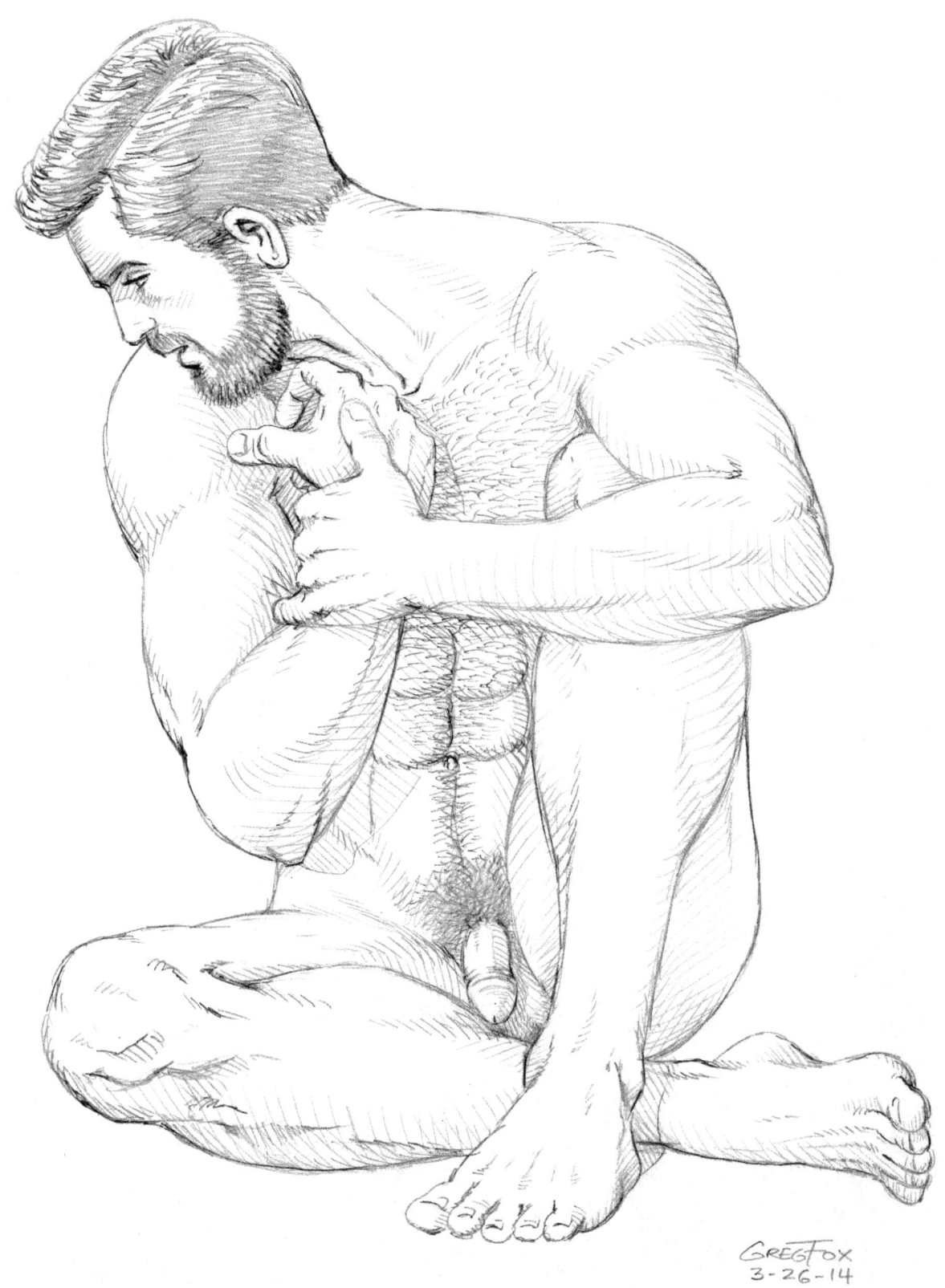

GregFox
3-26-14

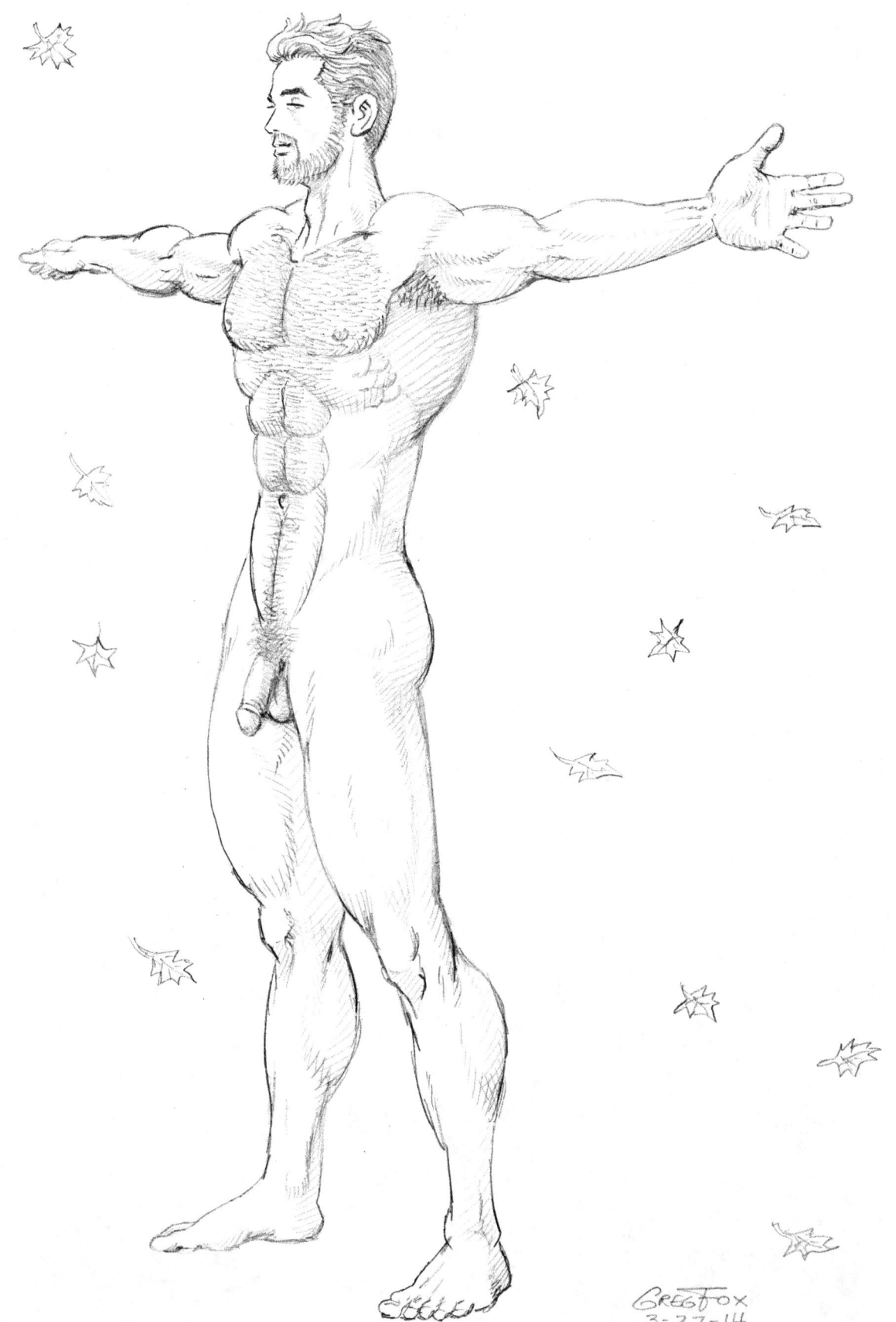

GregFox
3-27-14

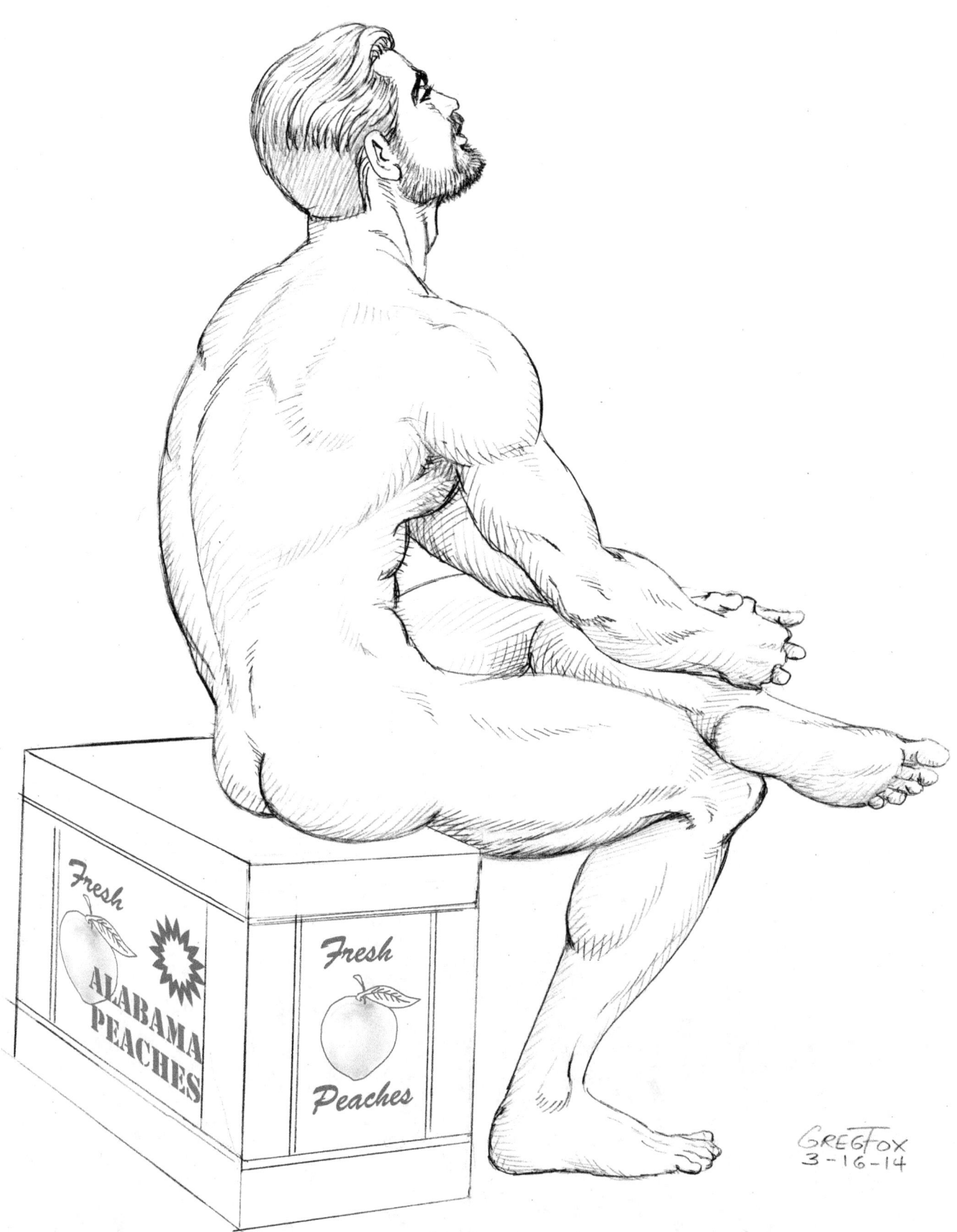

Fresh

ALABAMA
PEACHES

Fresh

Peaches

GregFox
3-16-14

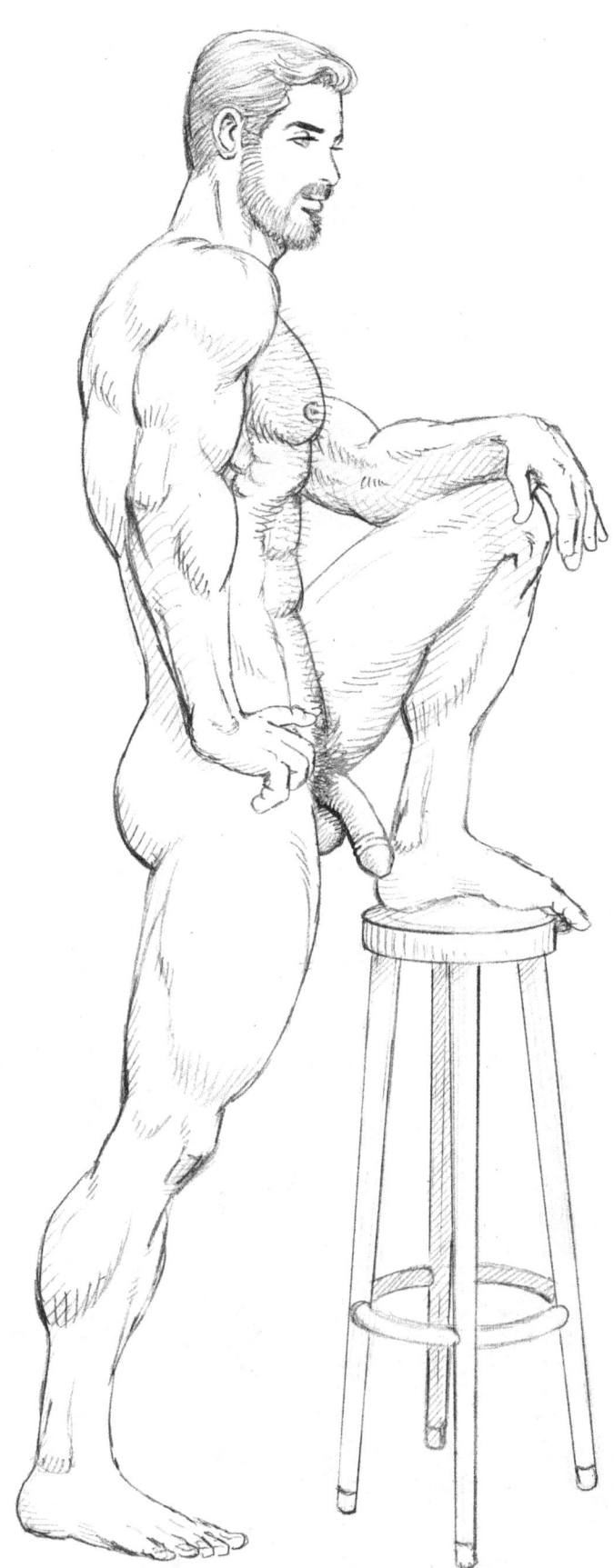

GregFox
3-10-14

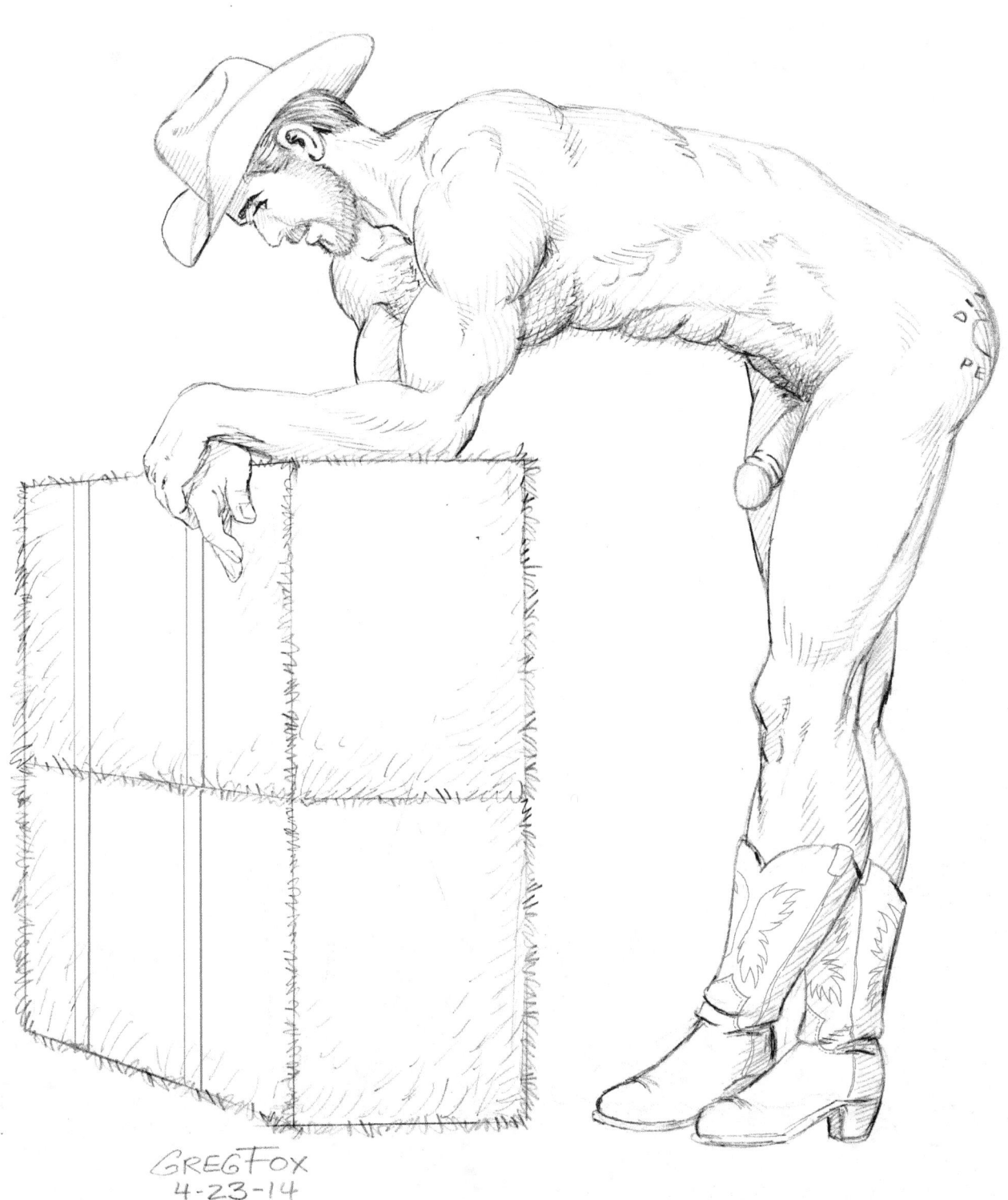

GregFox
4-23-14

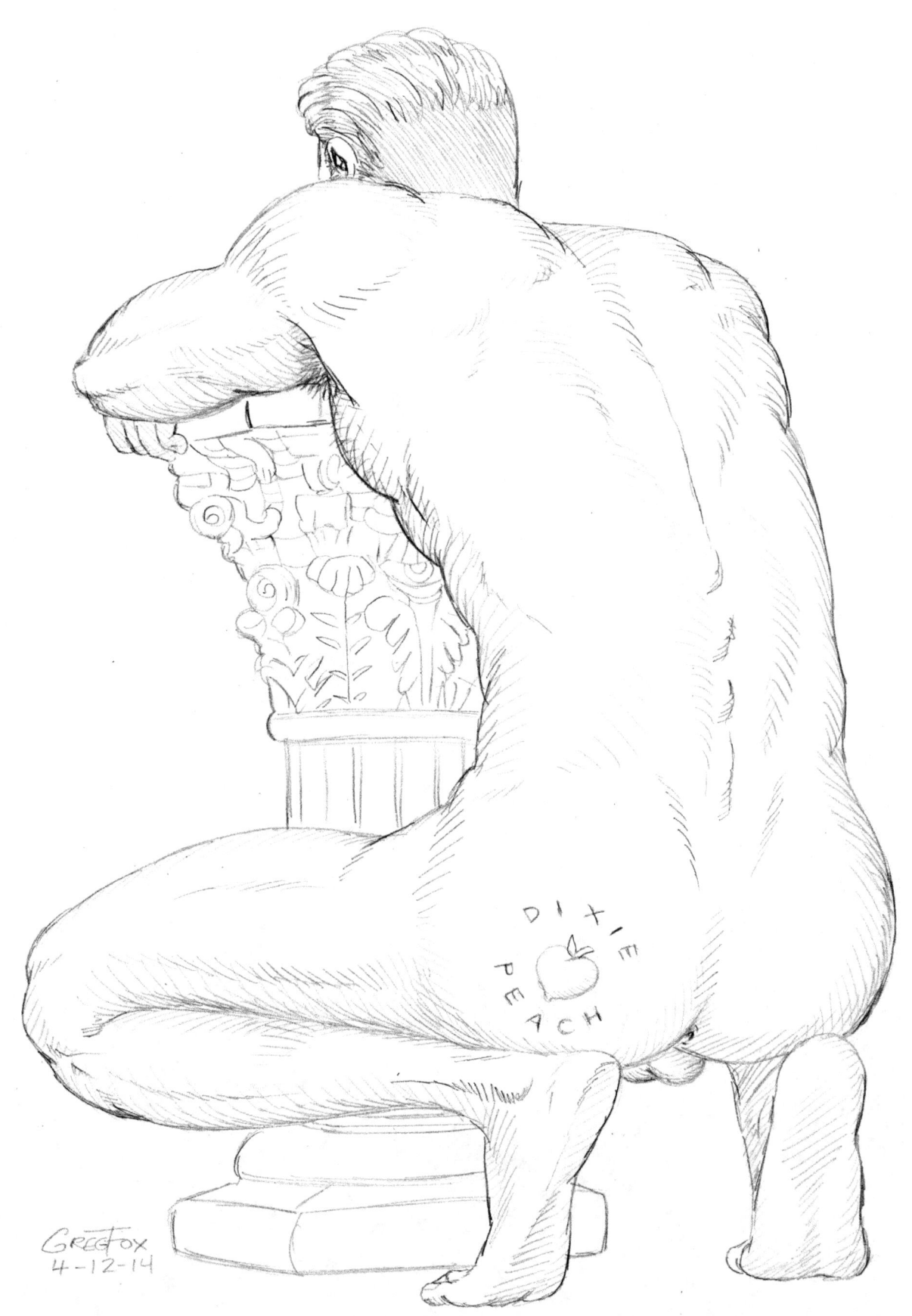

GregFox
4-12-14

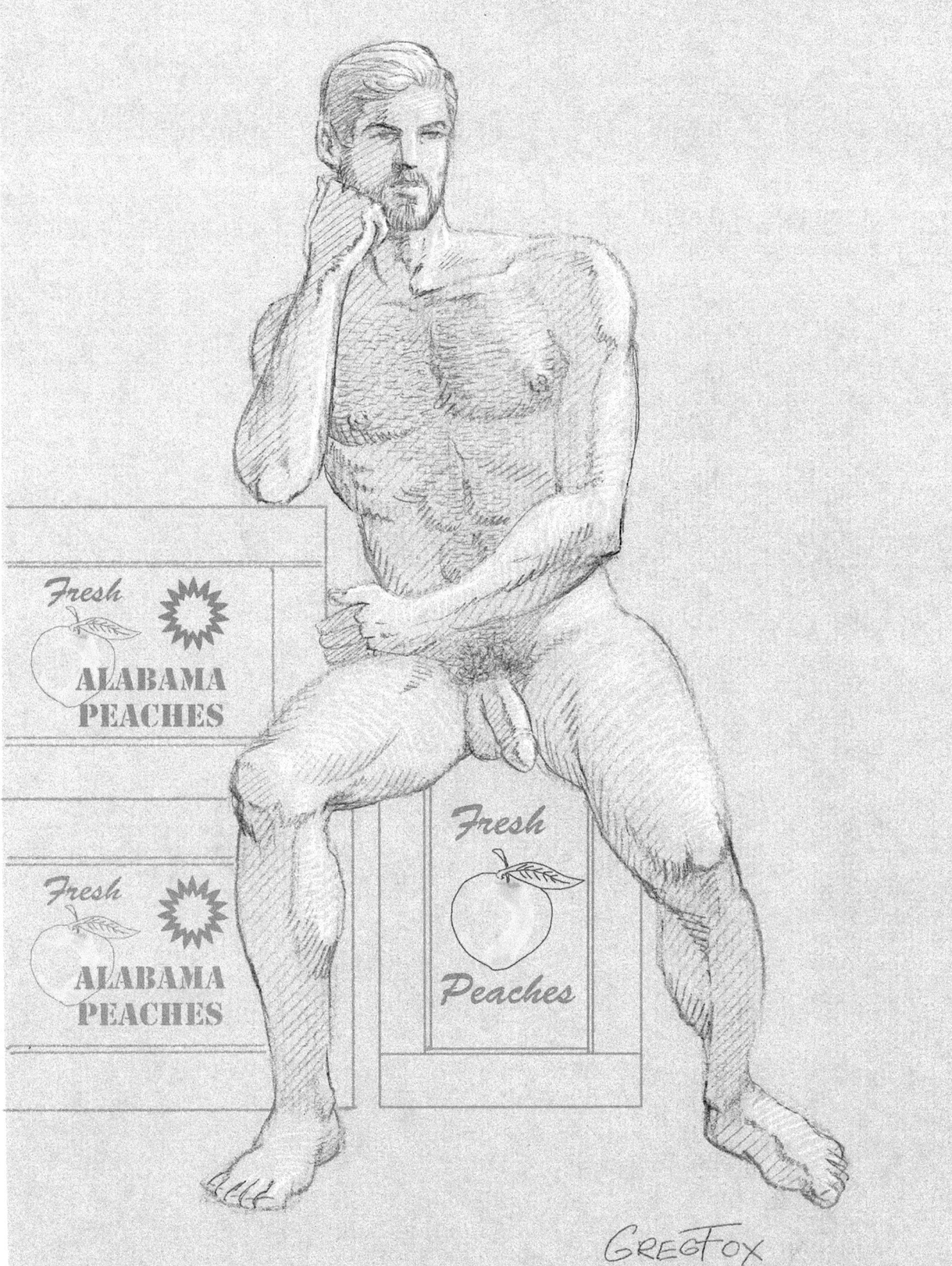

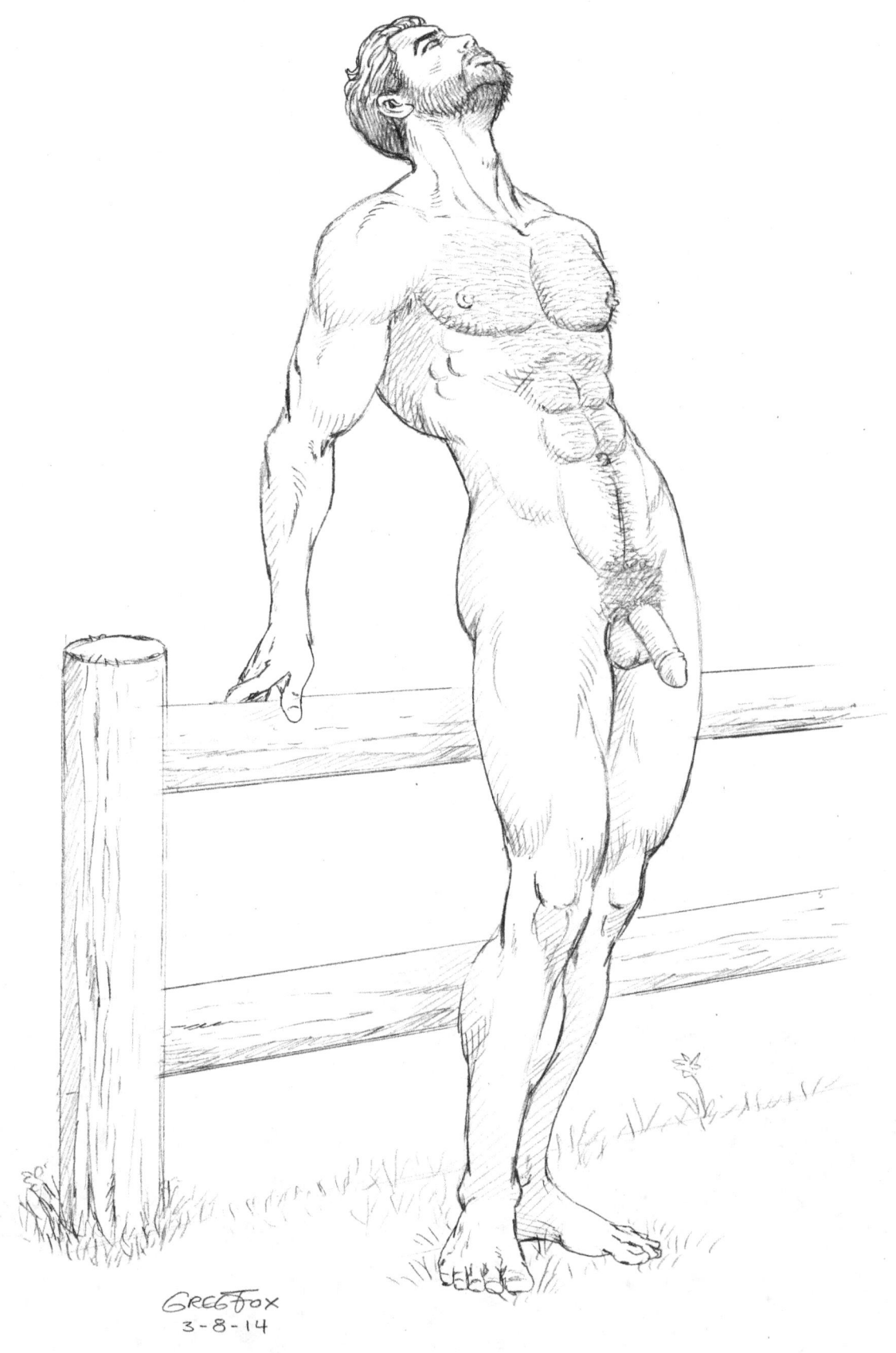

GregFox
3-8-14

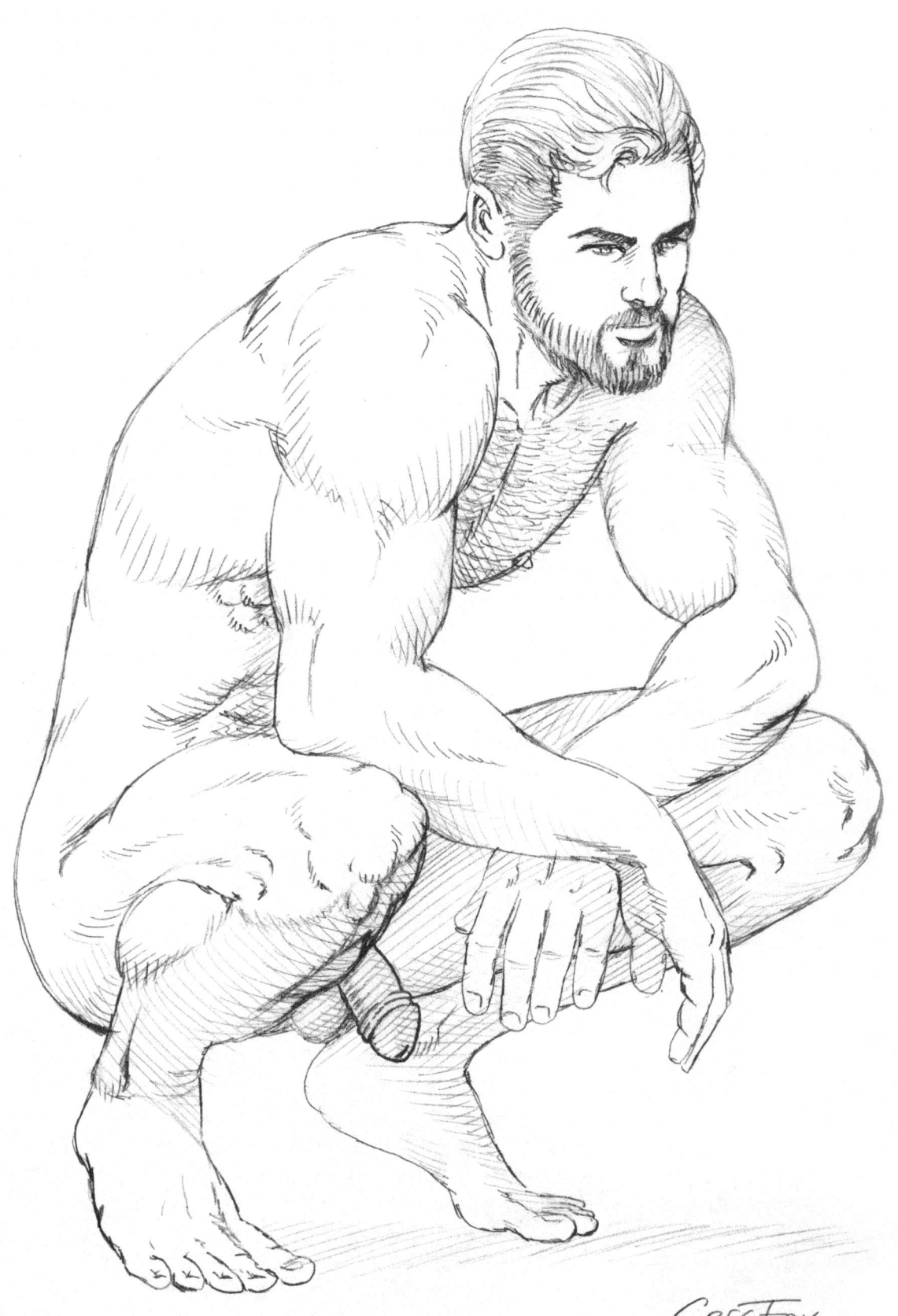

GregFox
3-7-14

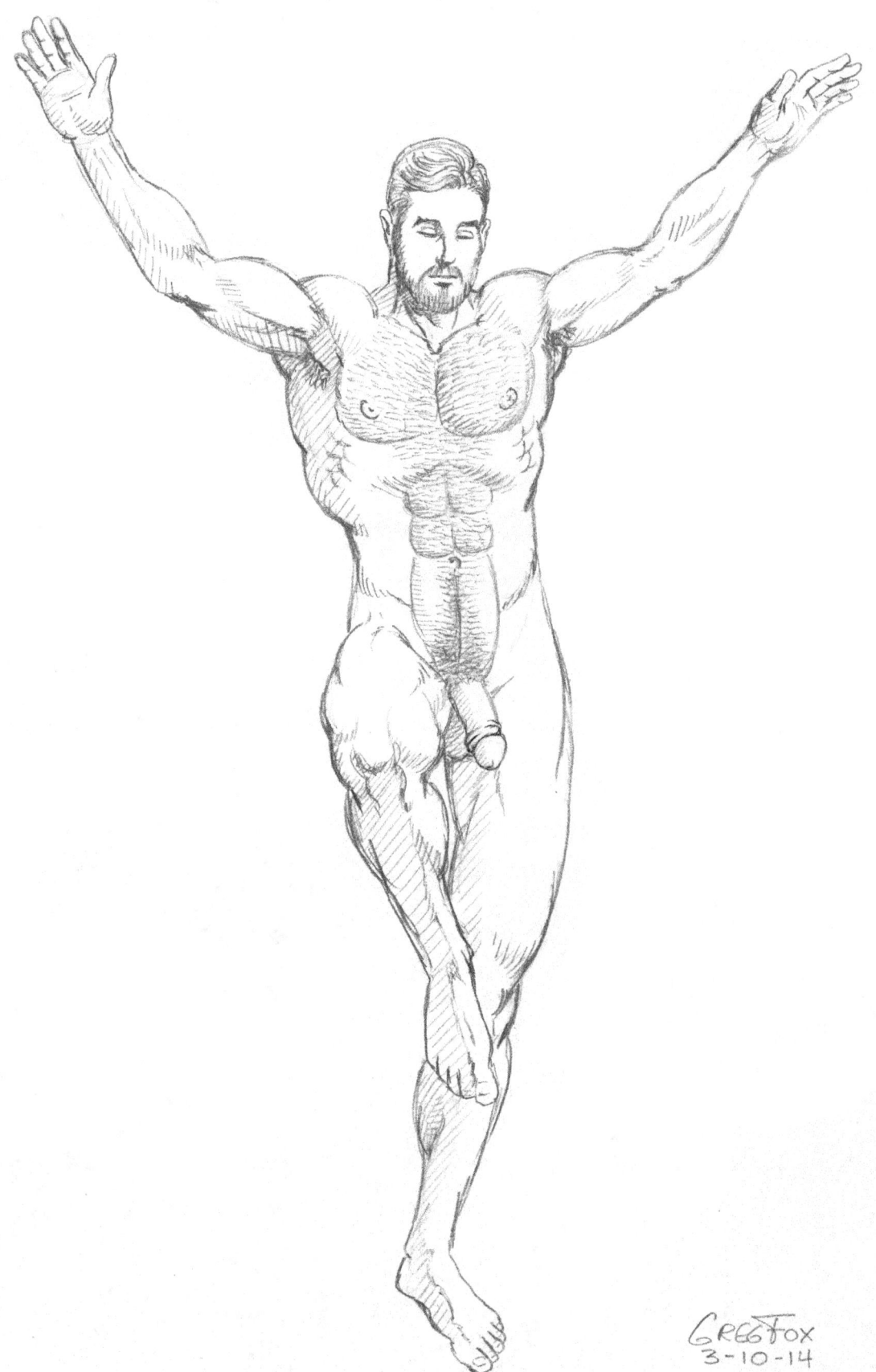

GregFox
3-10-14

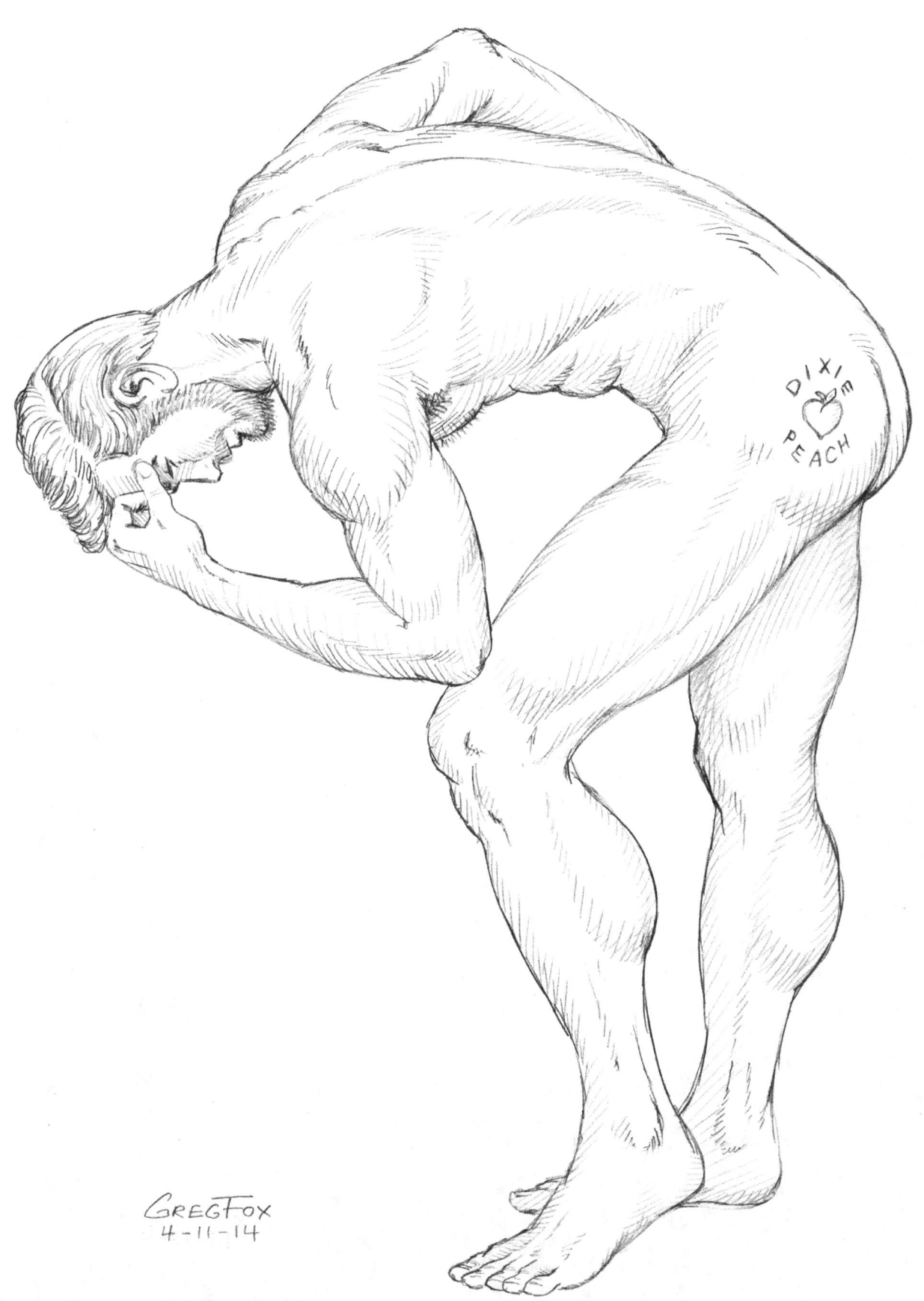

GregFox
4-11-14

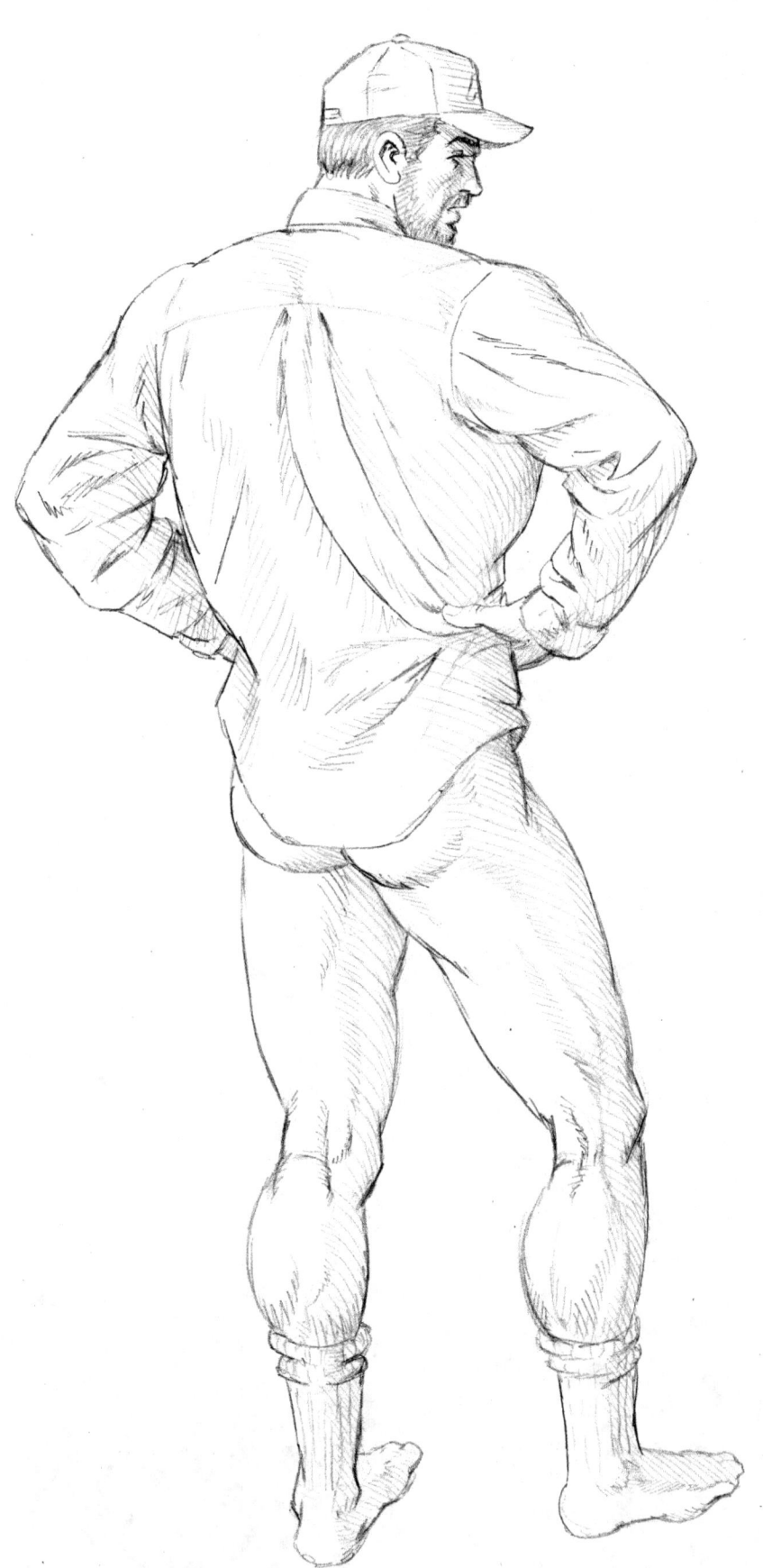

GregFox
4-24-14

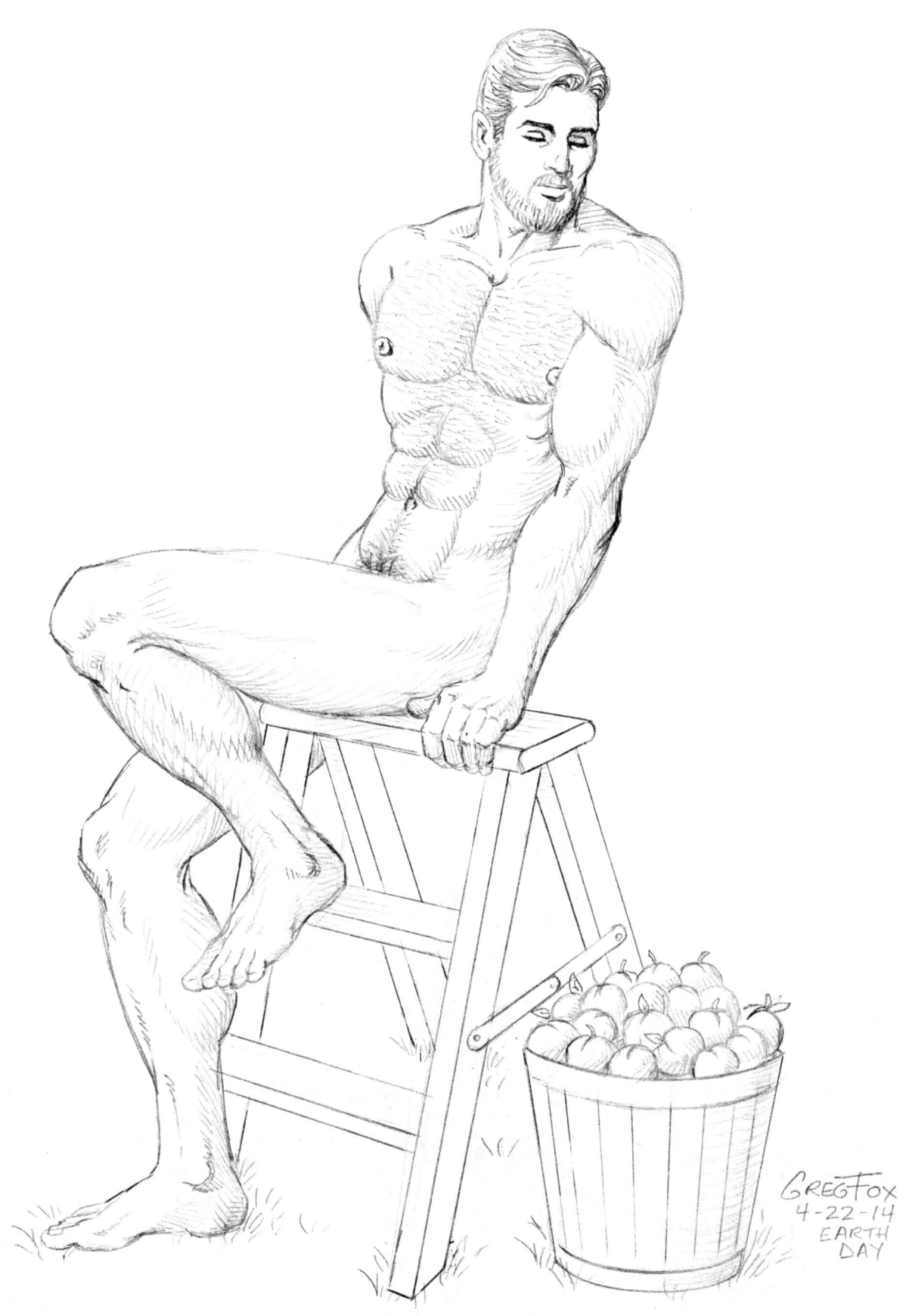

GregFox
4-22-14
EARTH
DAY

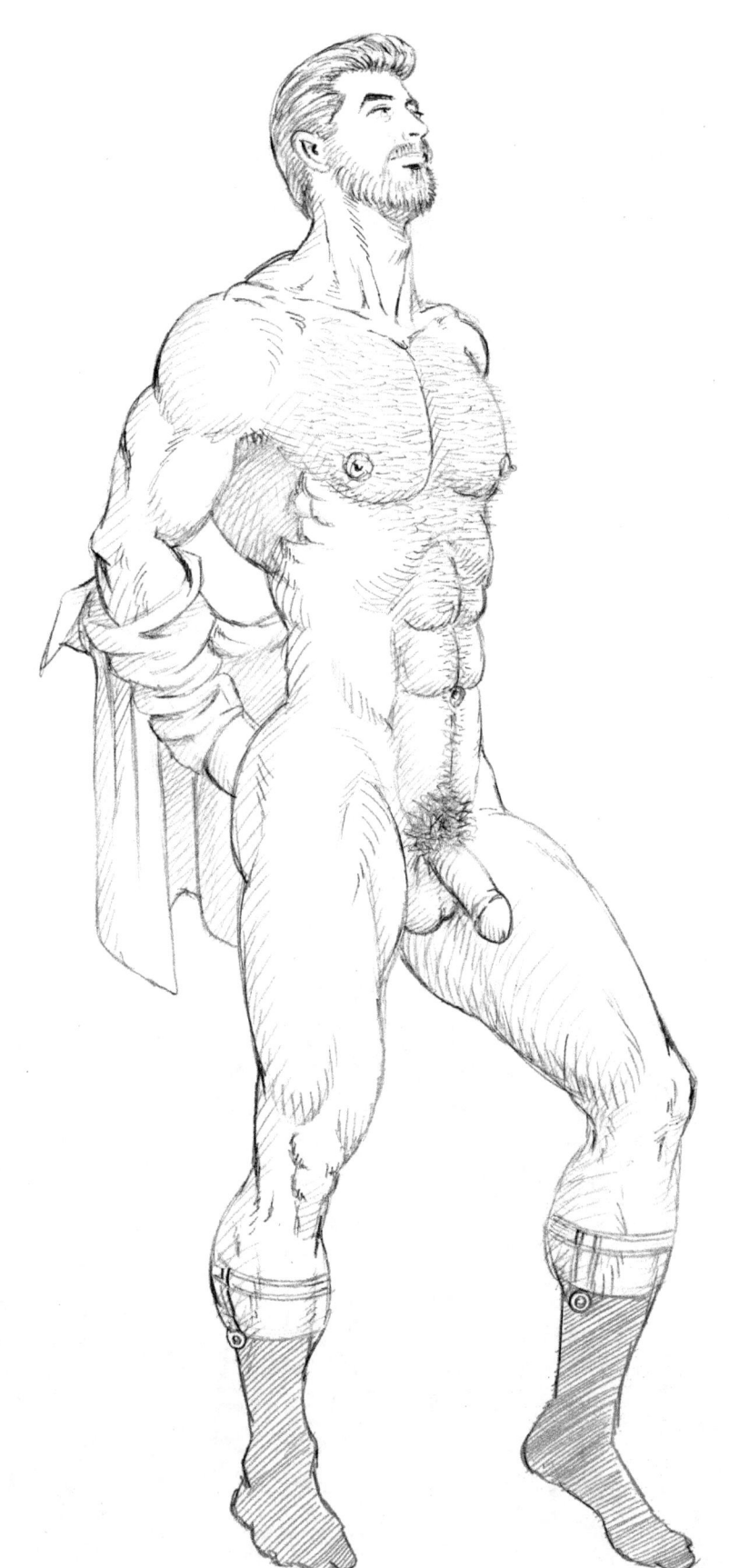

GregFox
4-7-14

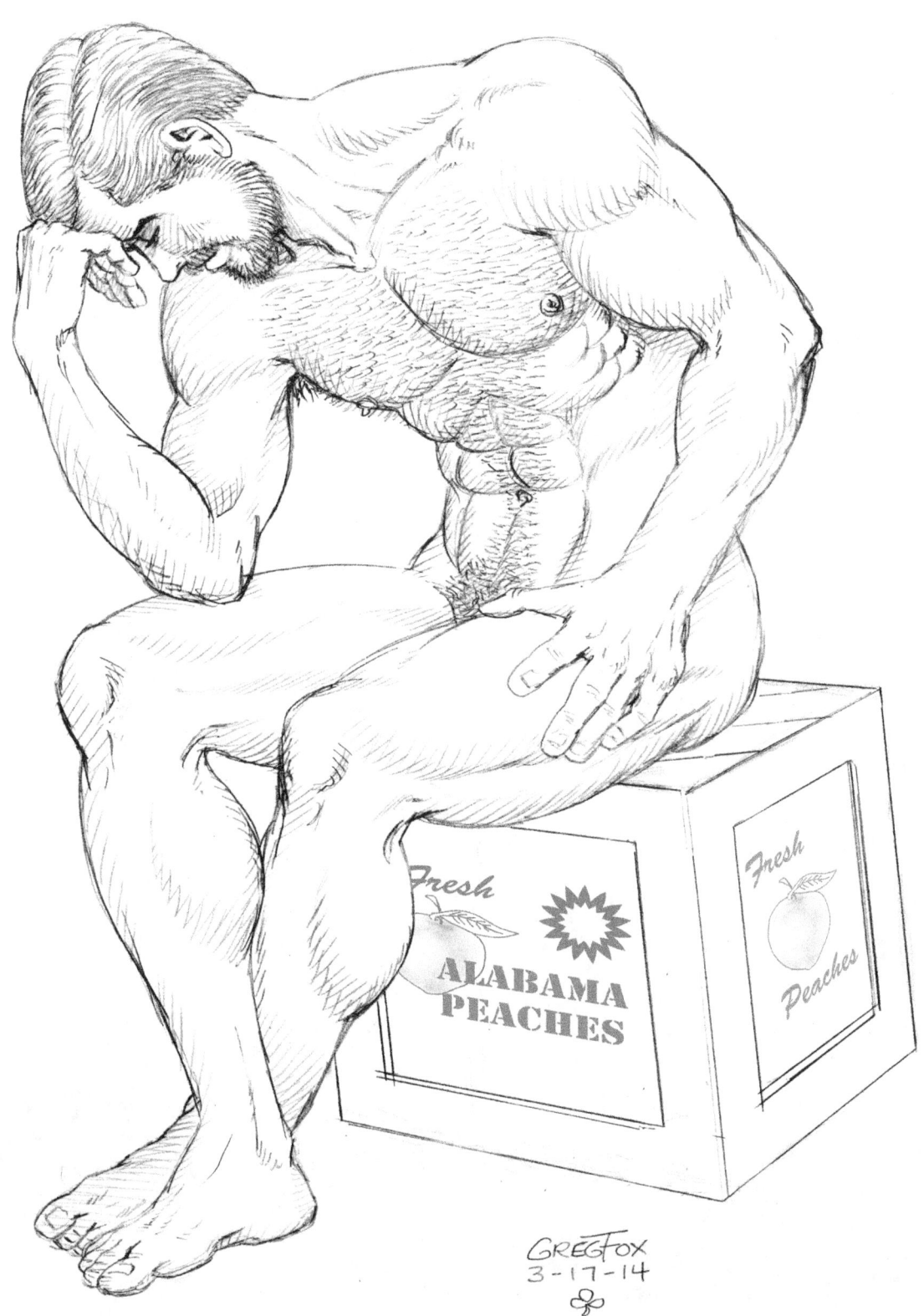

GREGFOX
3-17-14

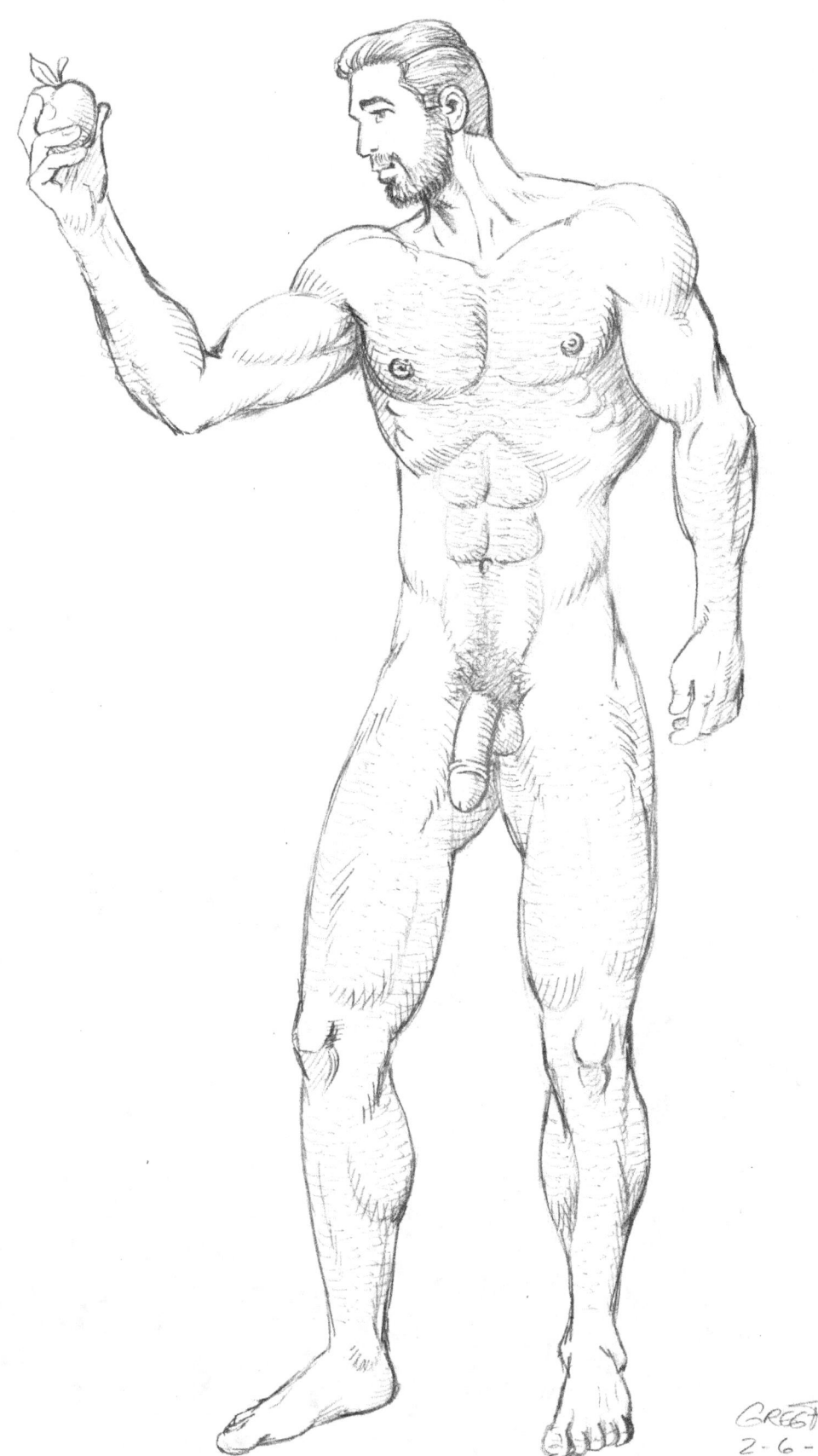

GregFox
2-6-14

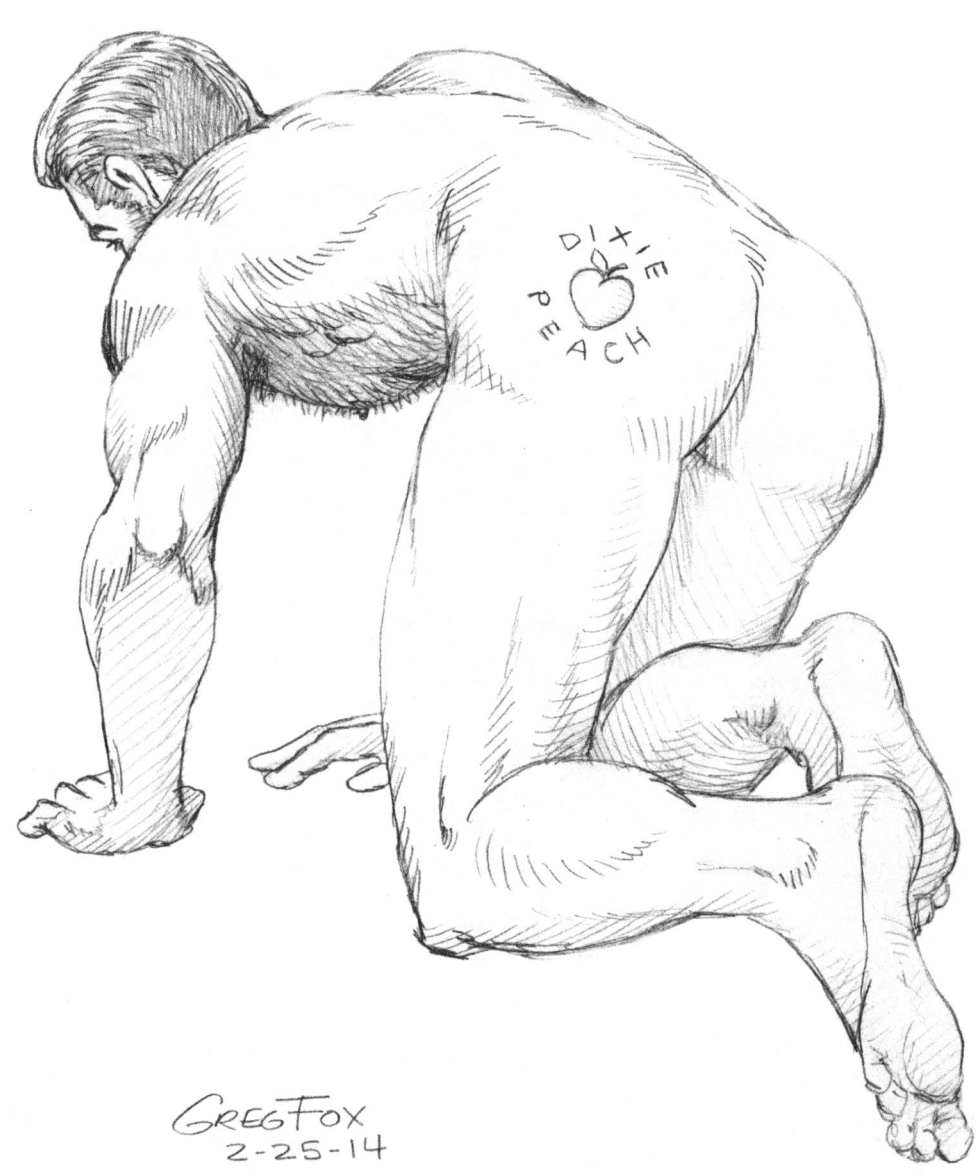

GregFox
2-25-14

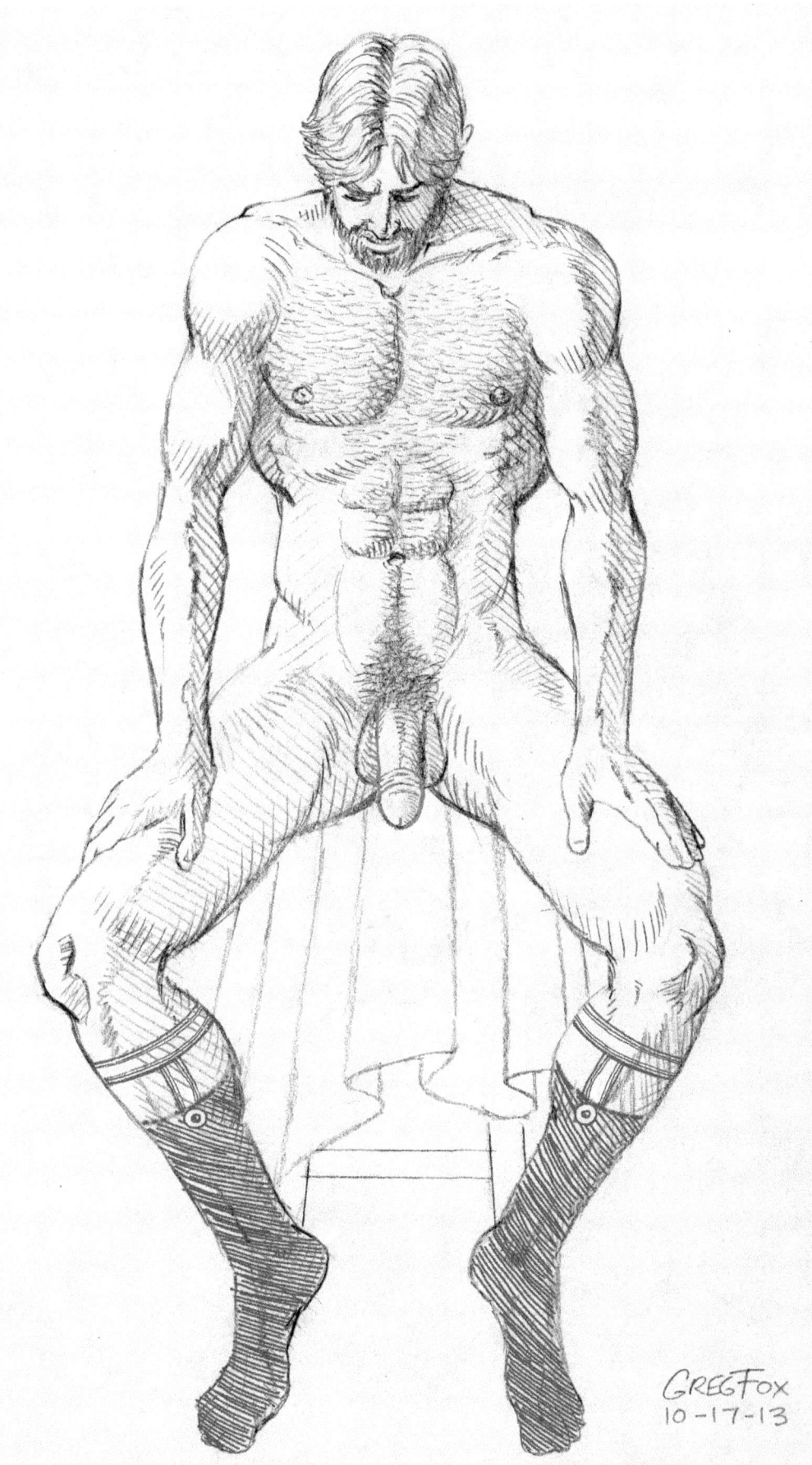

GregFox
10-17-13

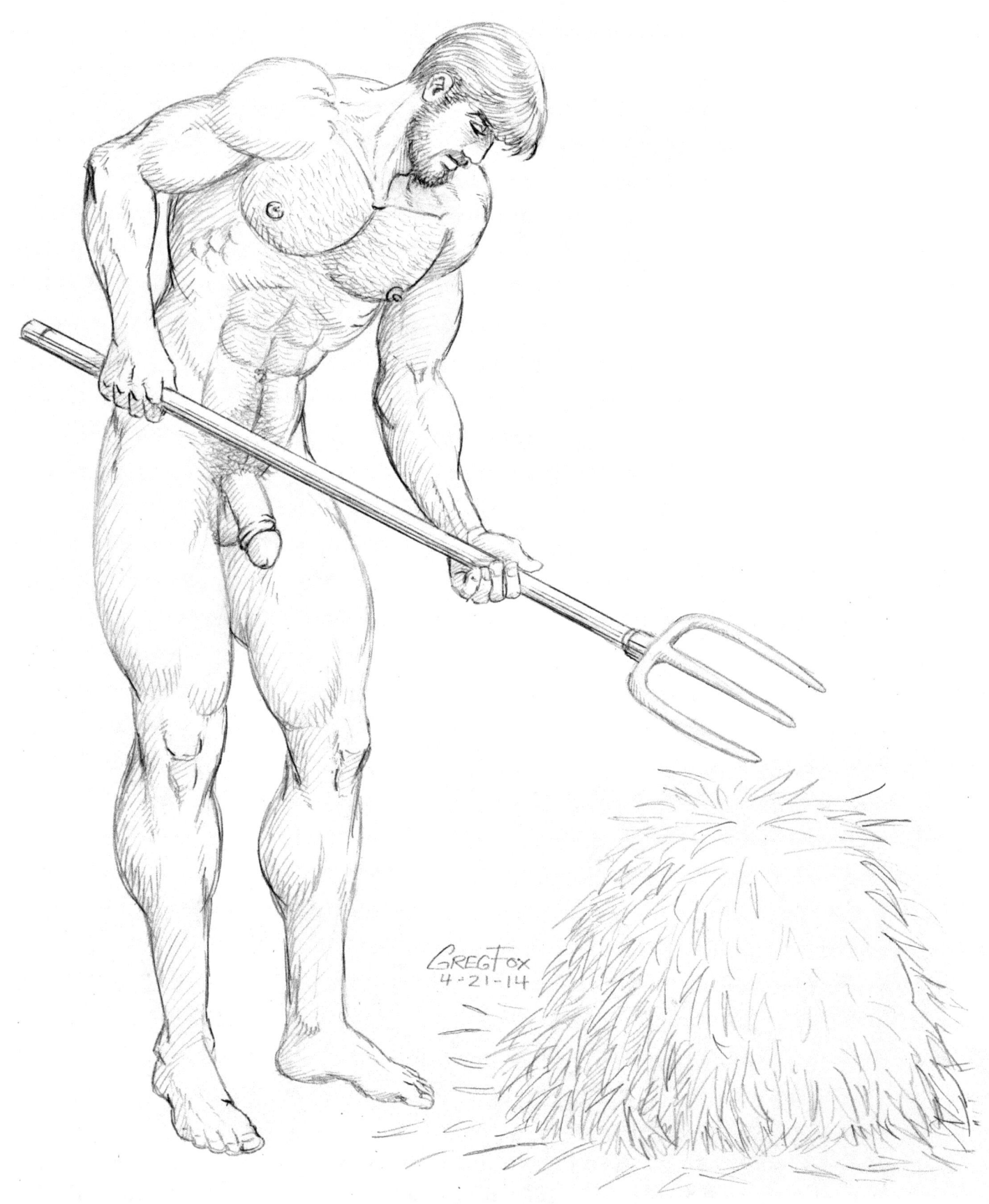

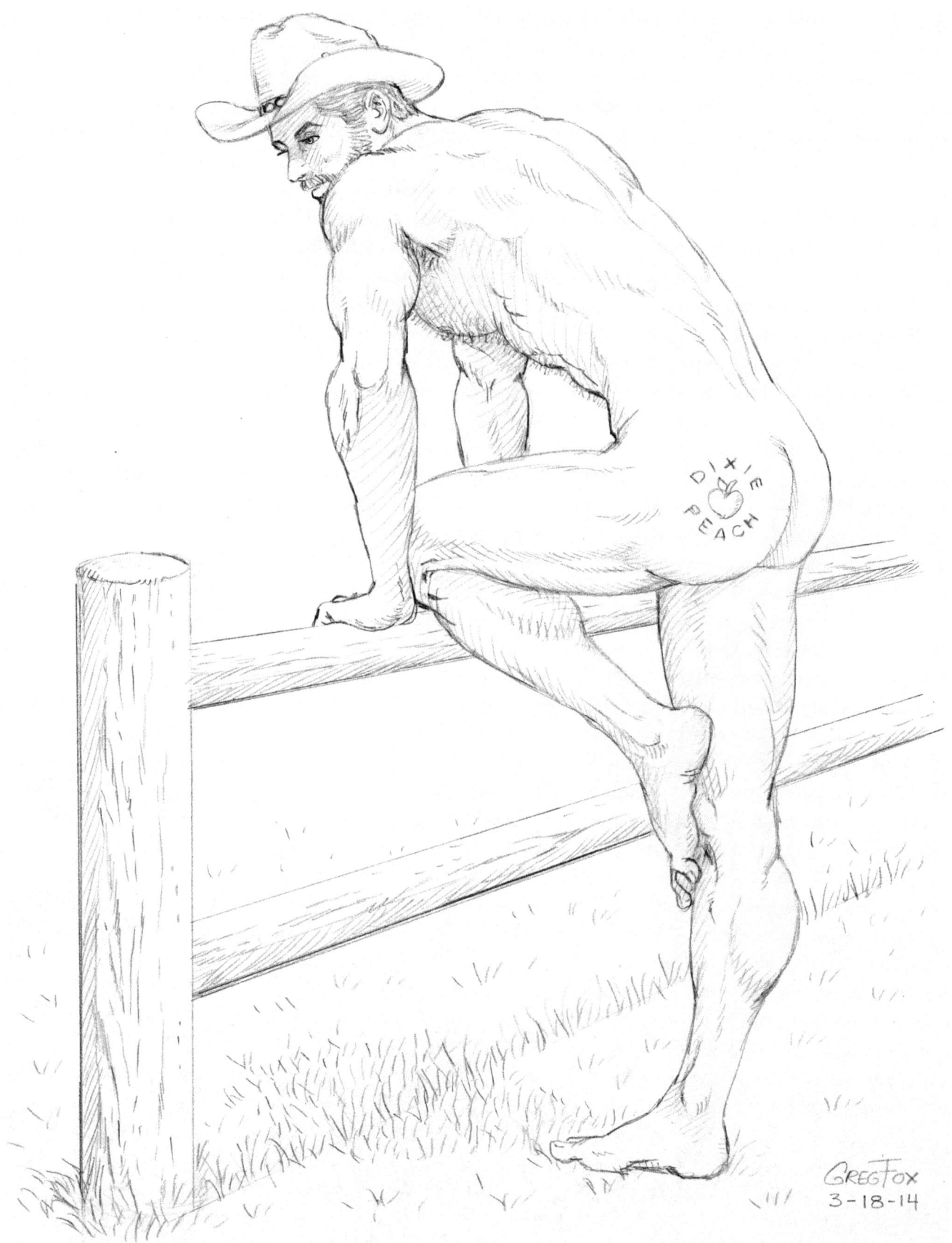

GregFox
3-18-14

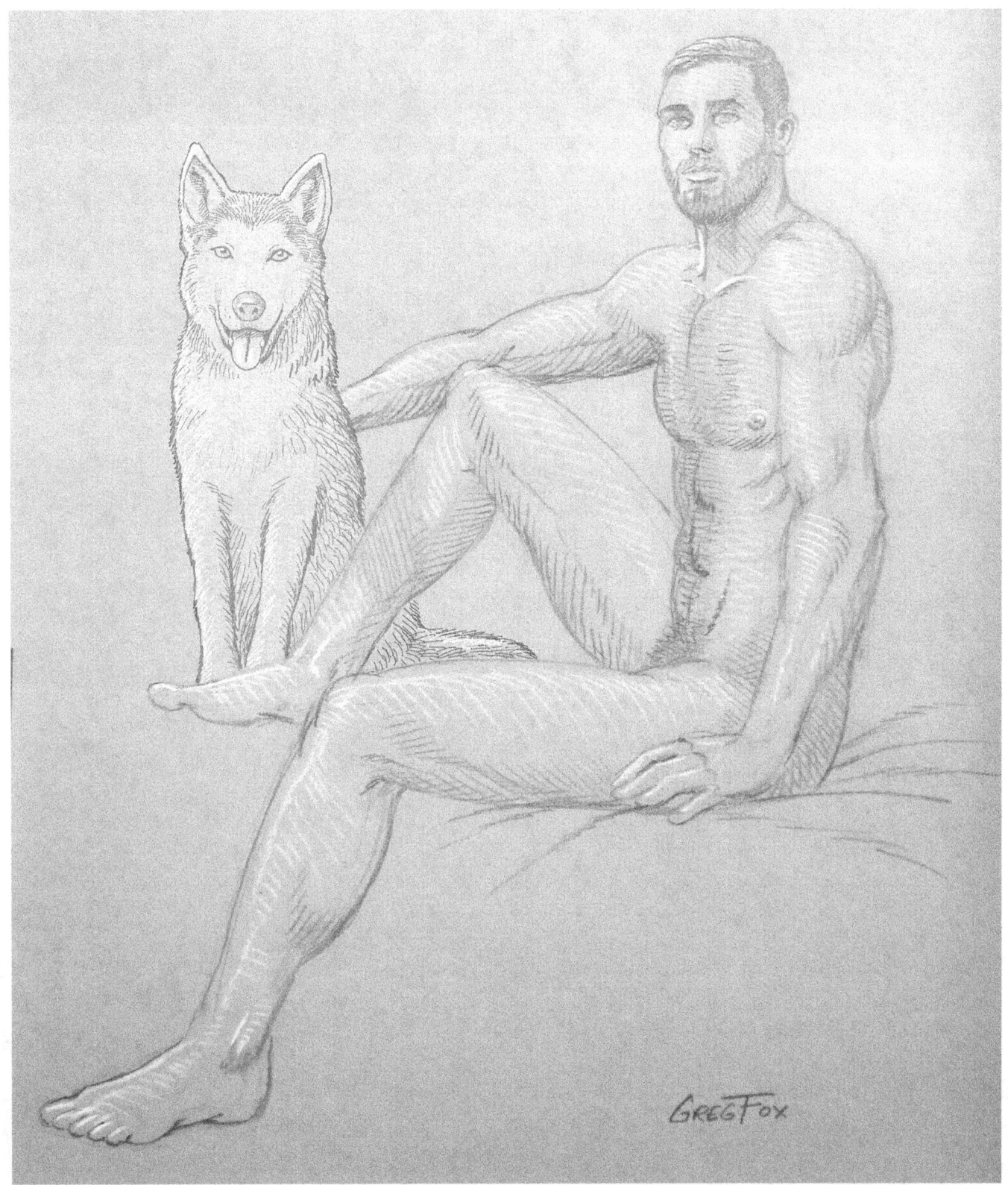

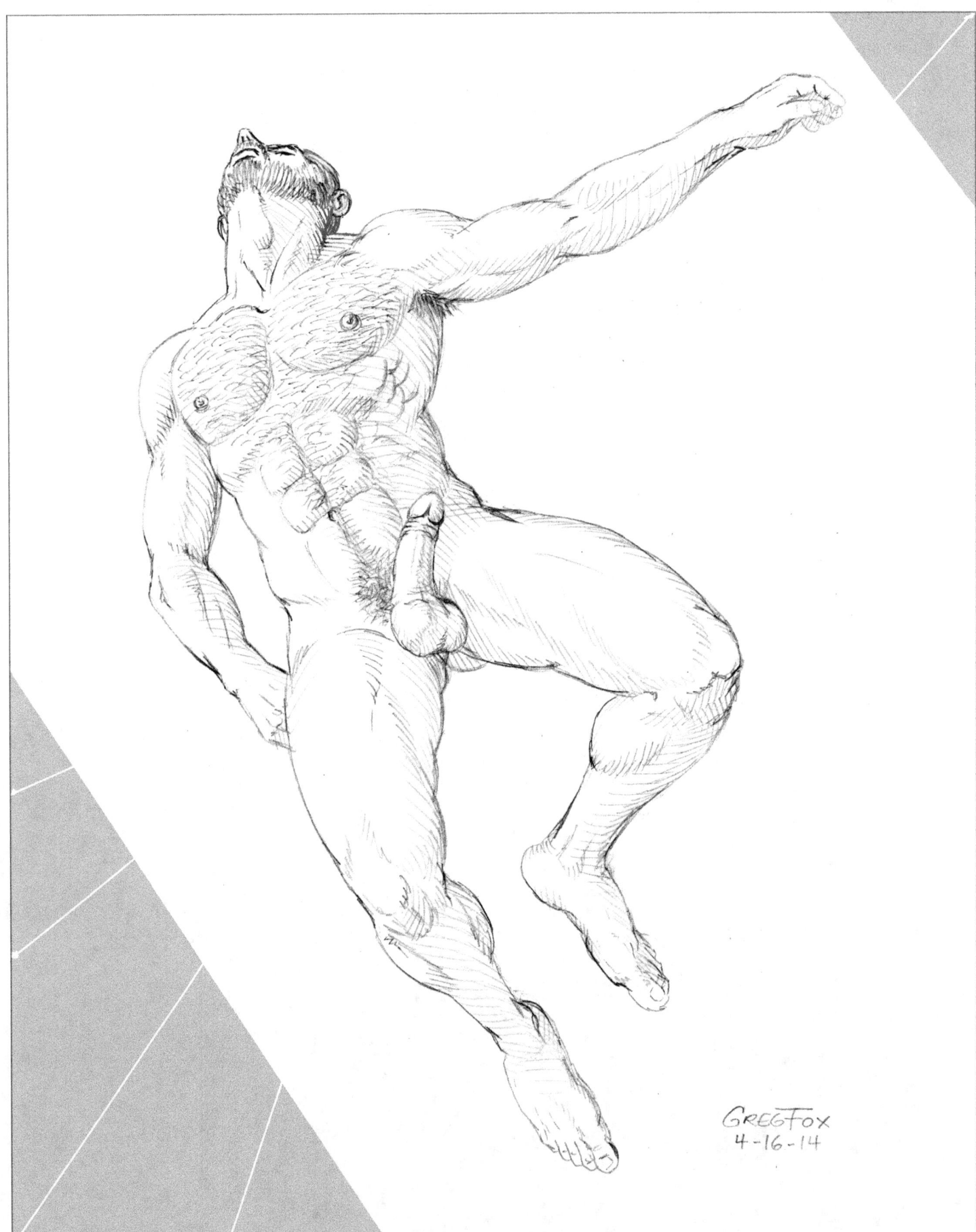

GregFox
4-16-14

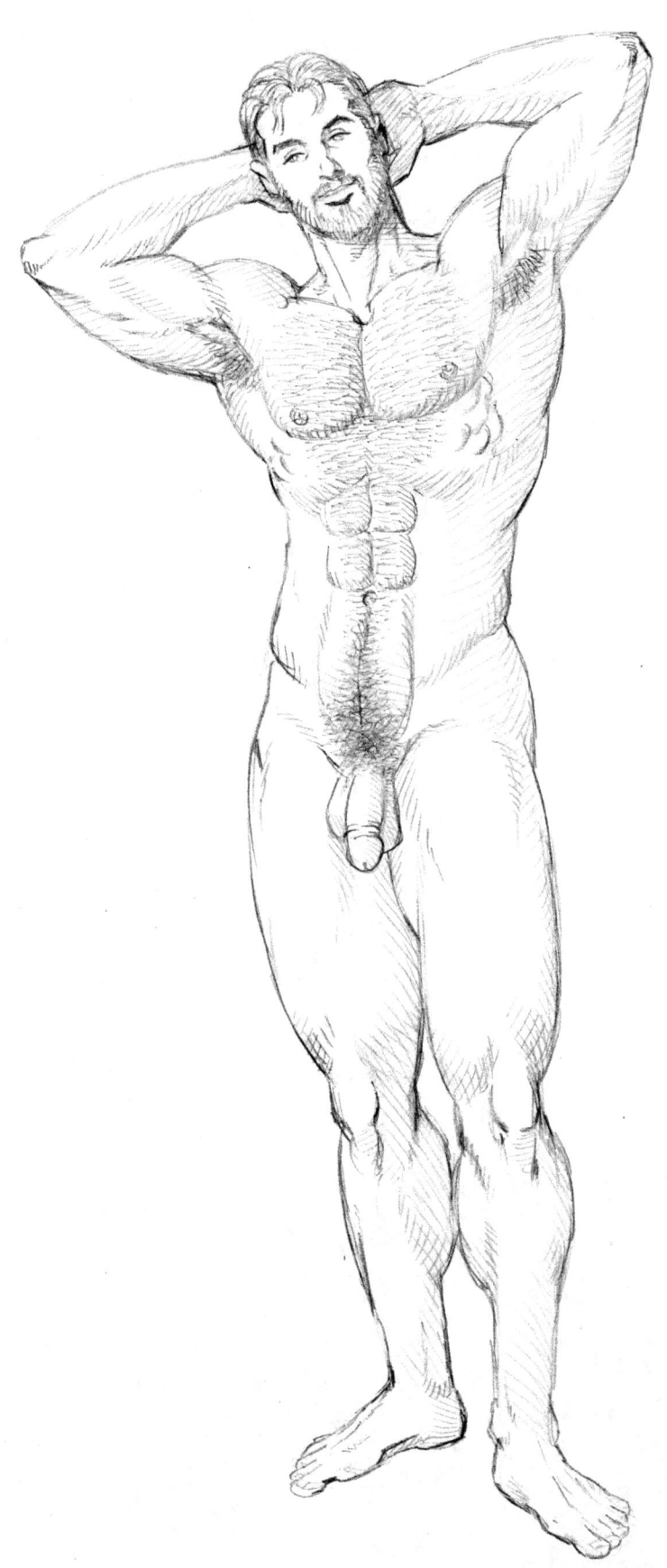

GregFox
4-4-14

Horizontal Drawings

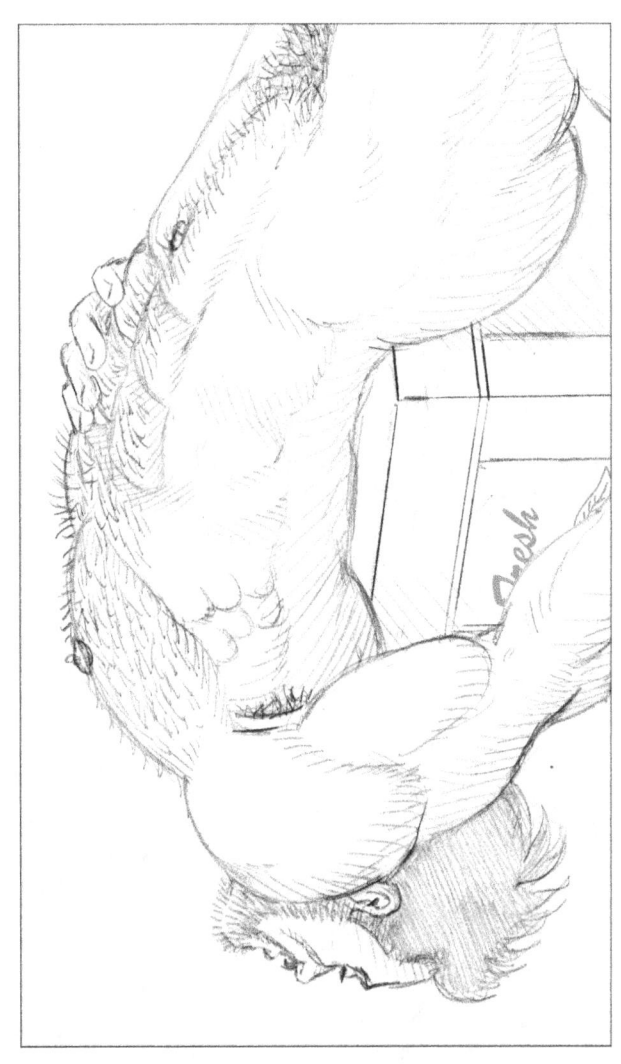

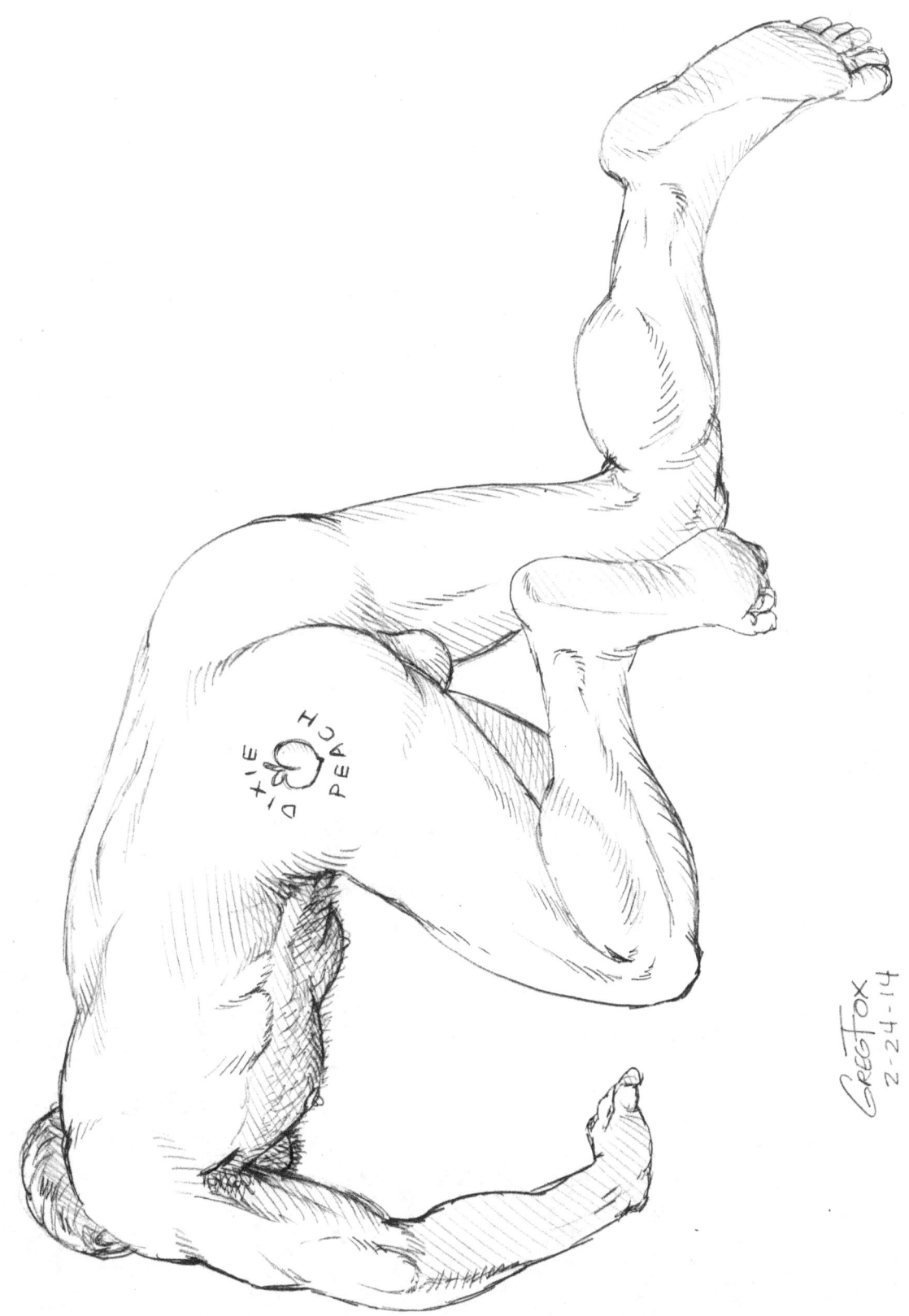

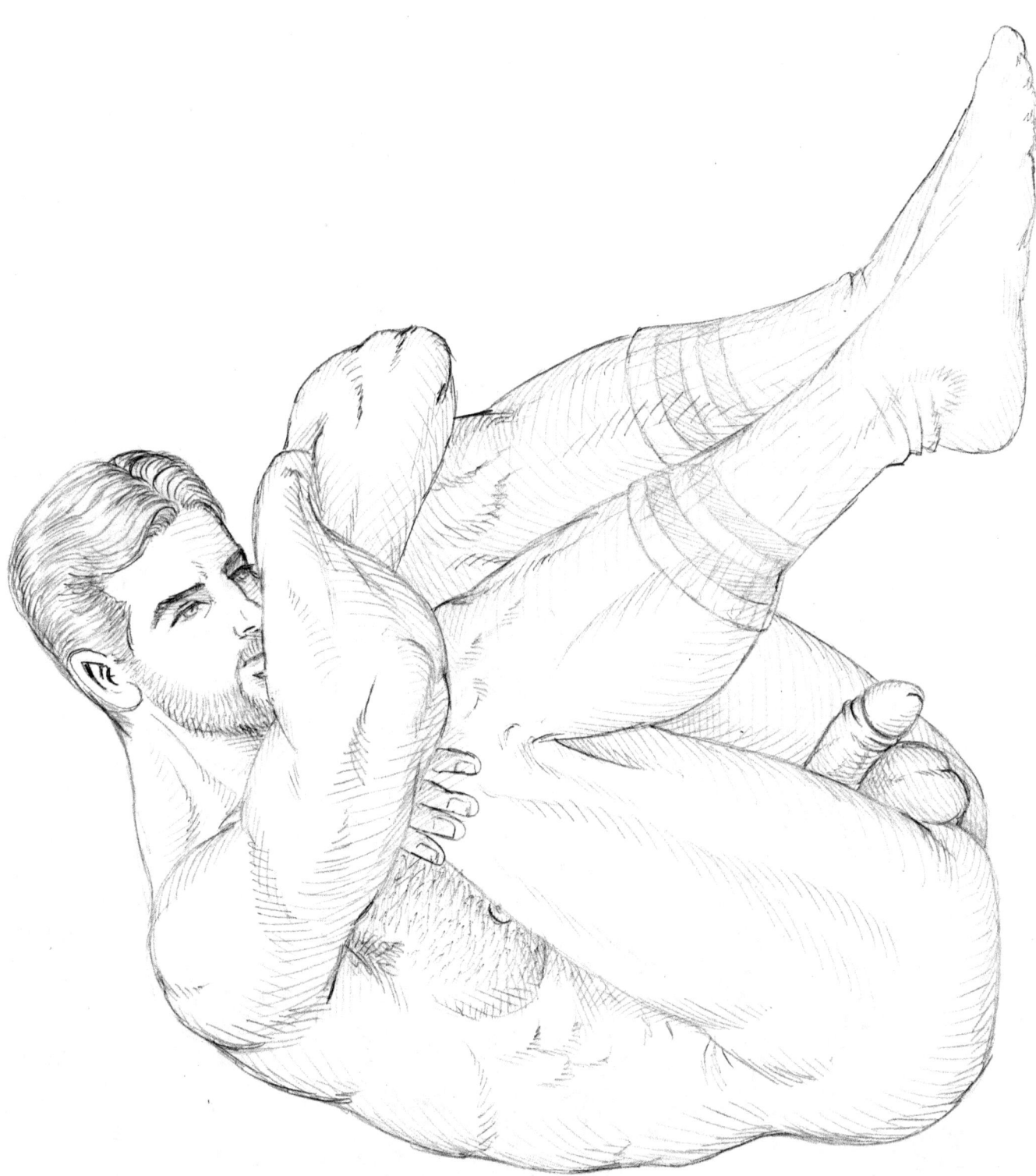

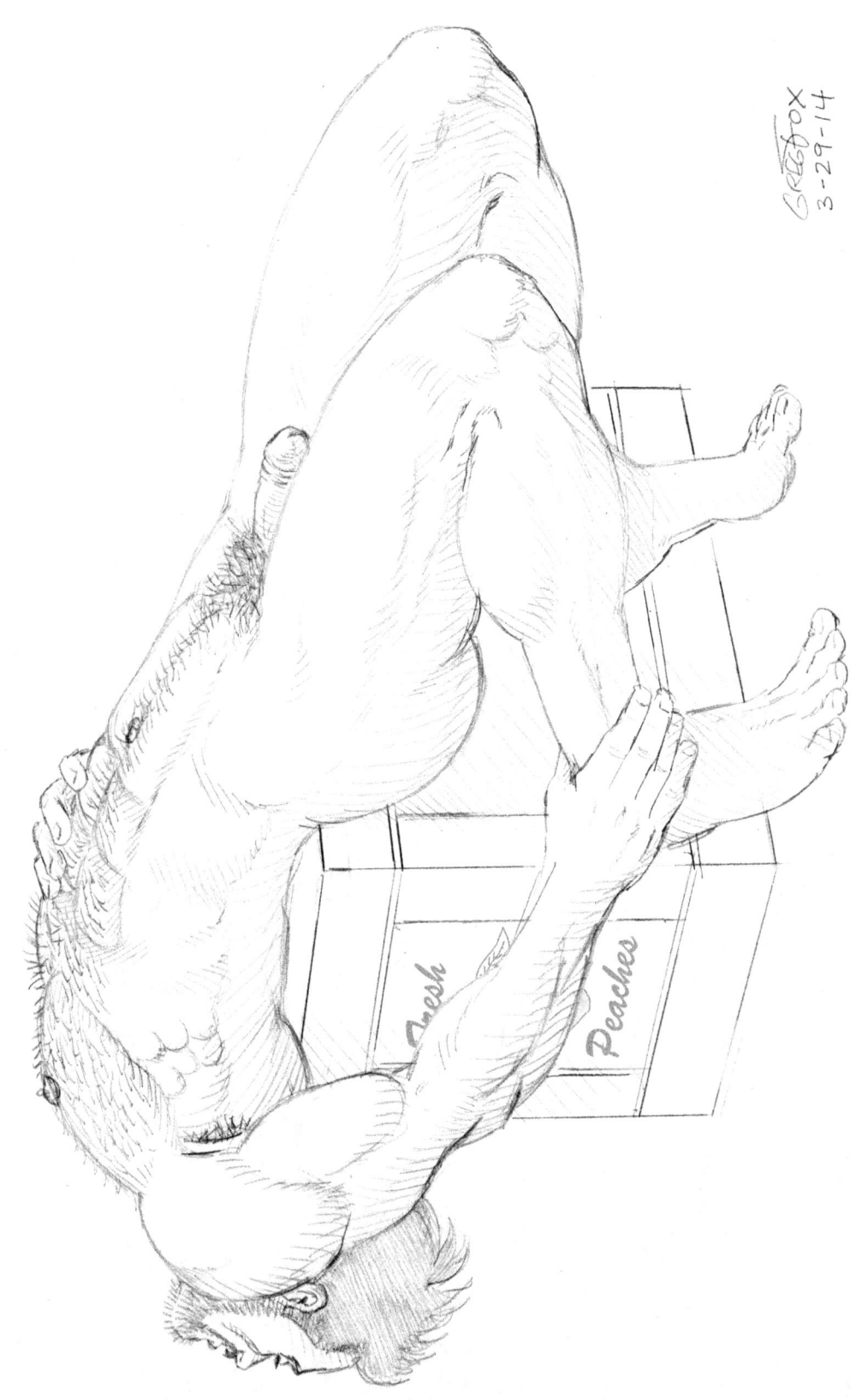

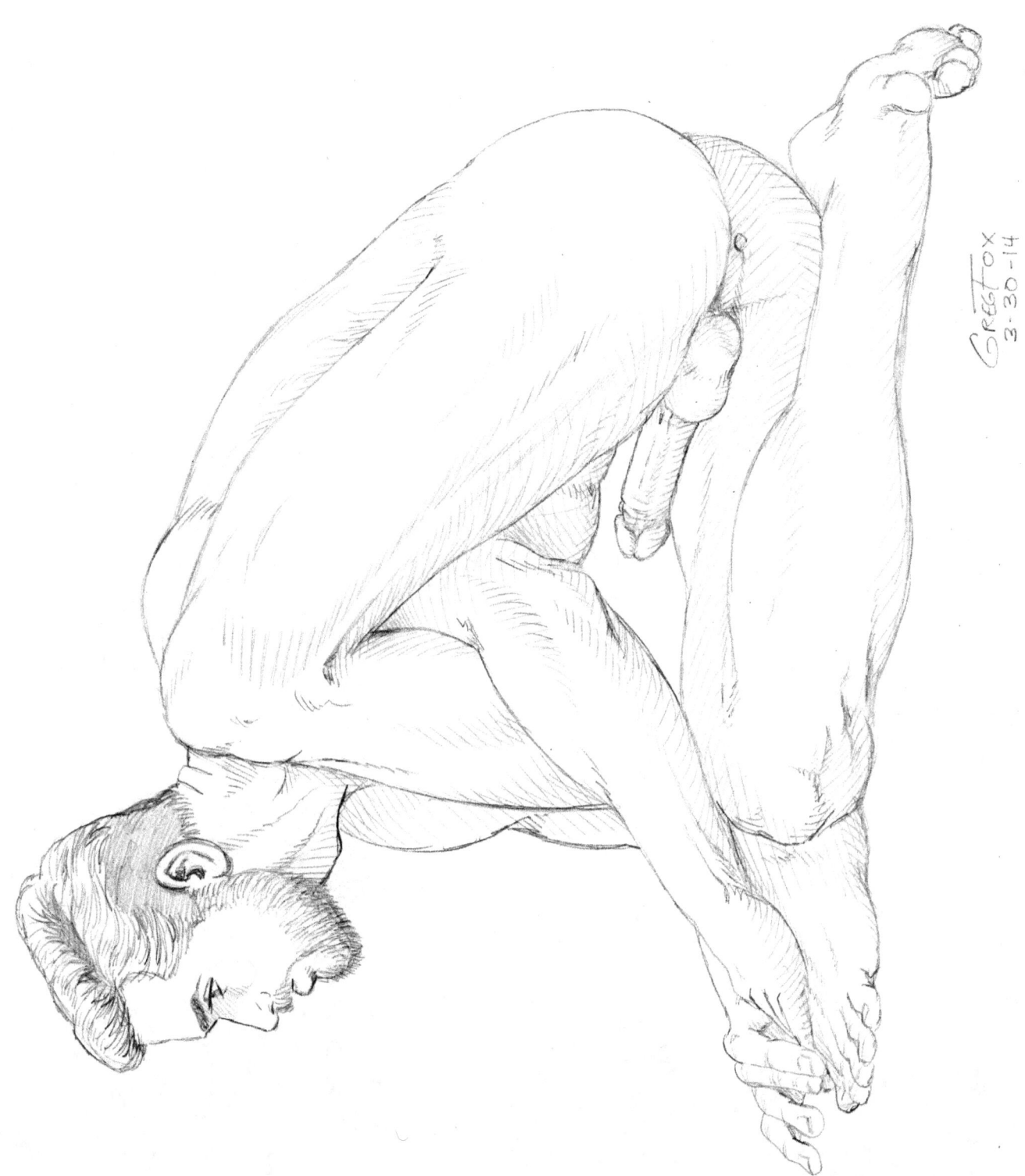

GreggFox
3-30-14

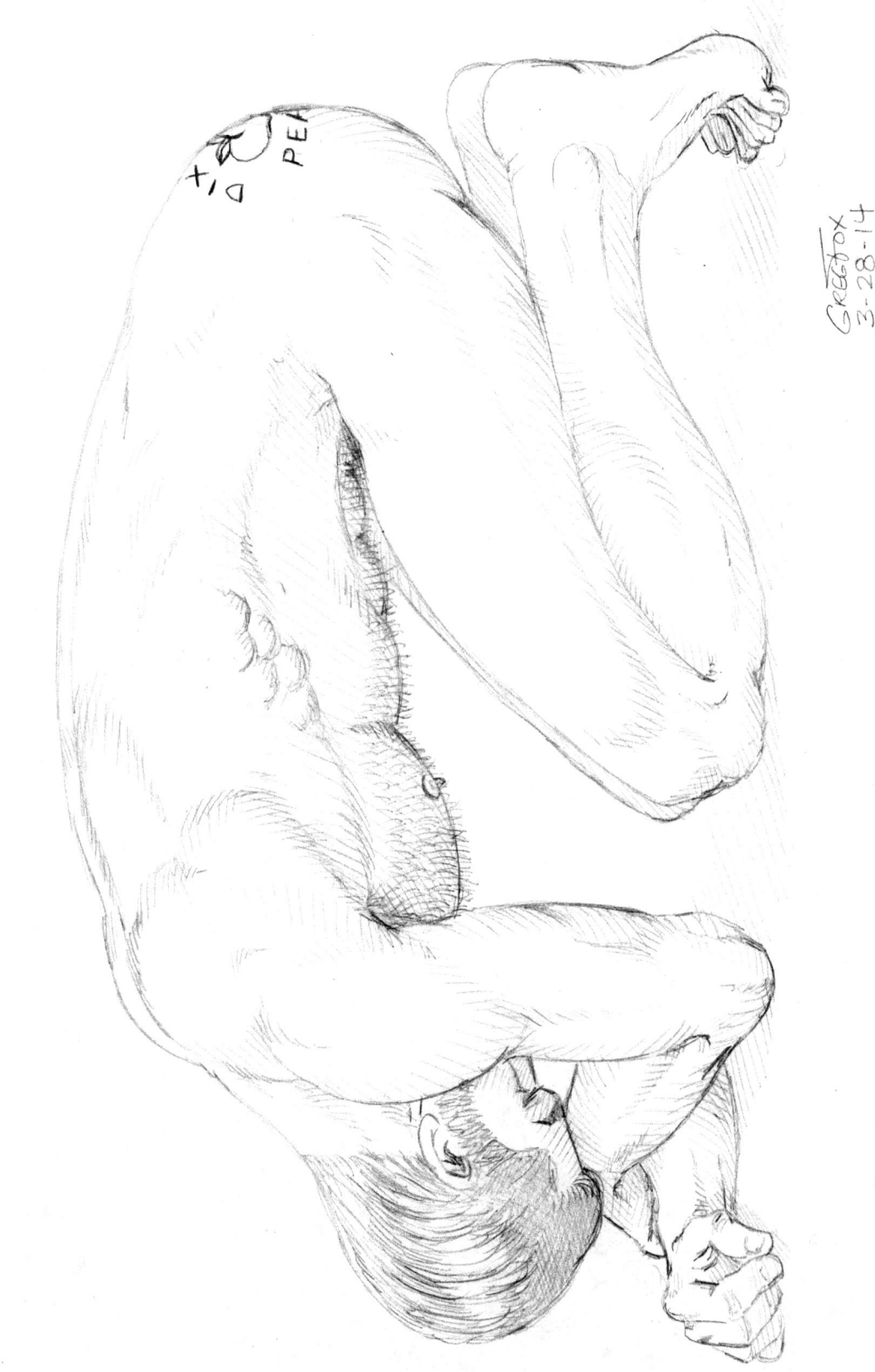

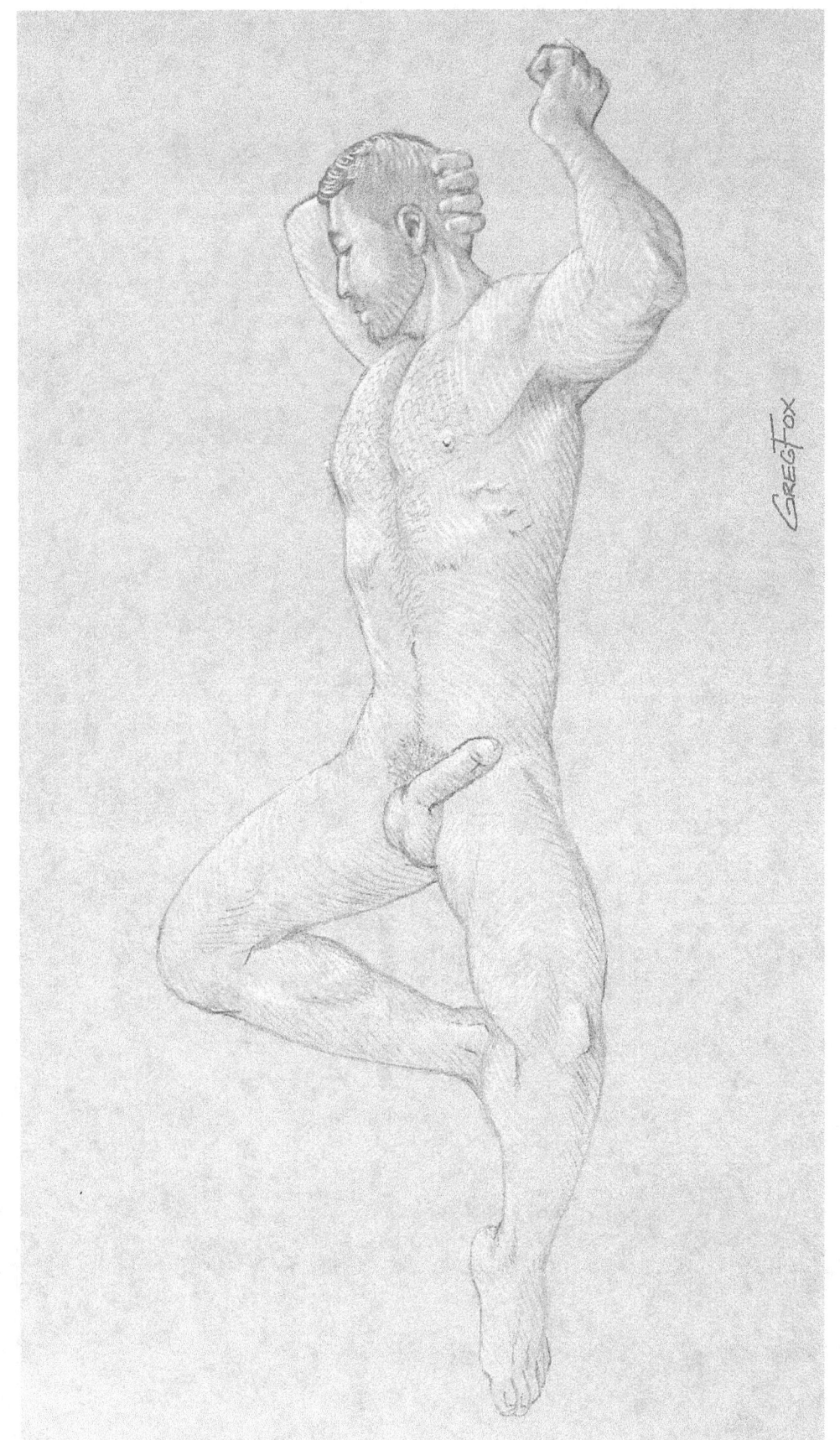

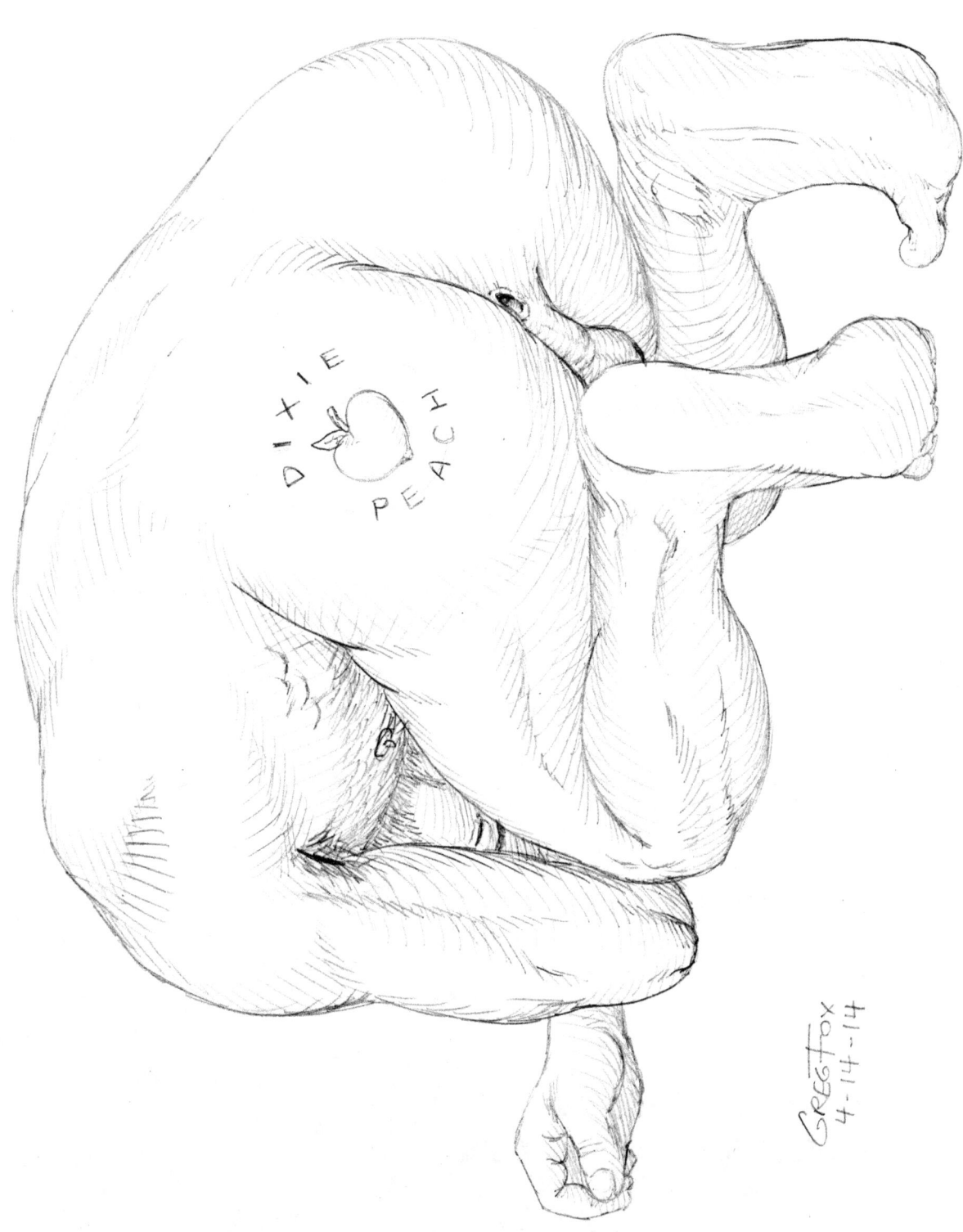

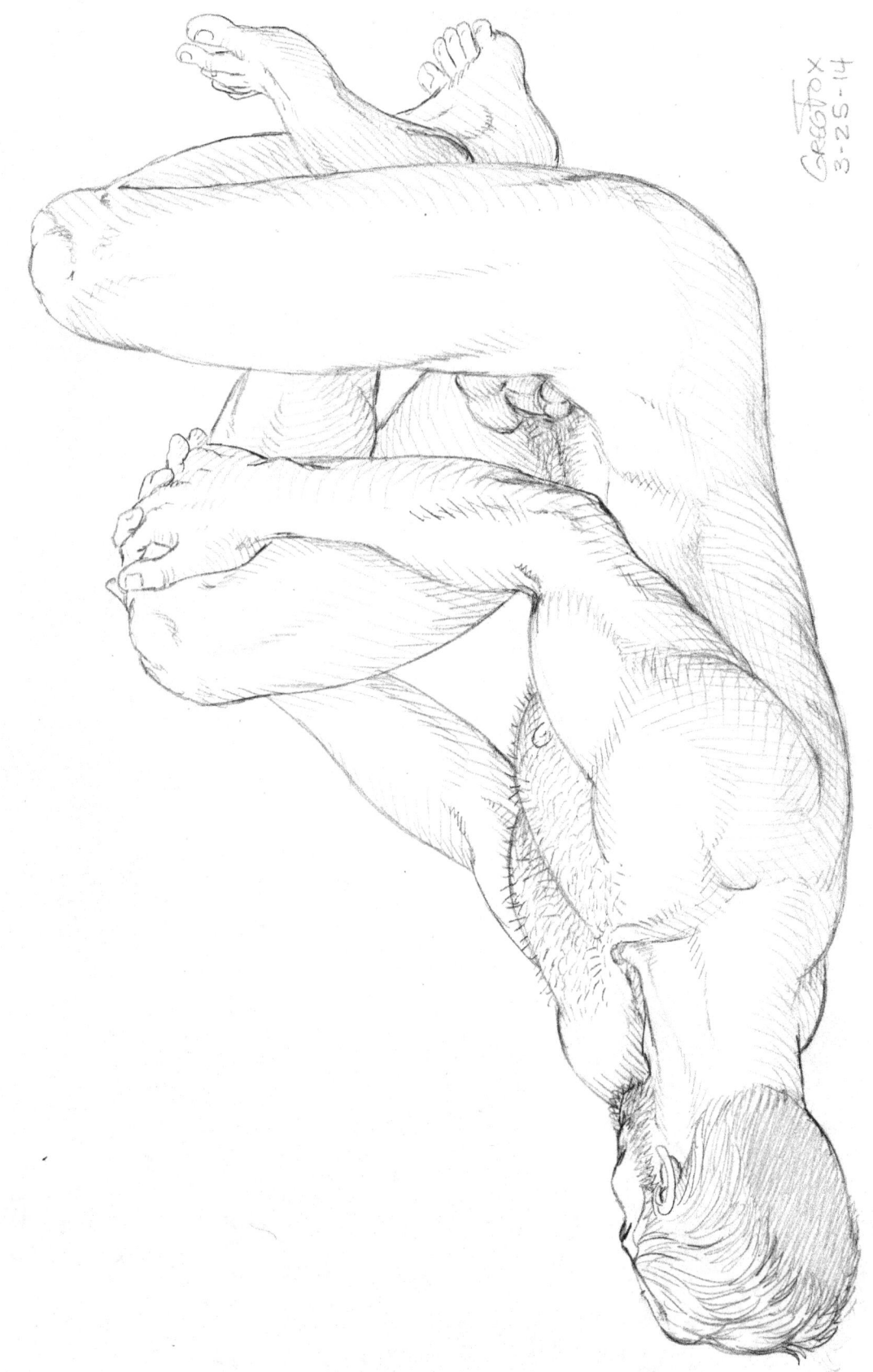

GregFox
3-25-14

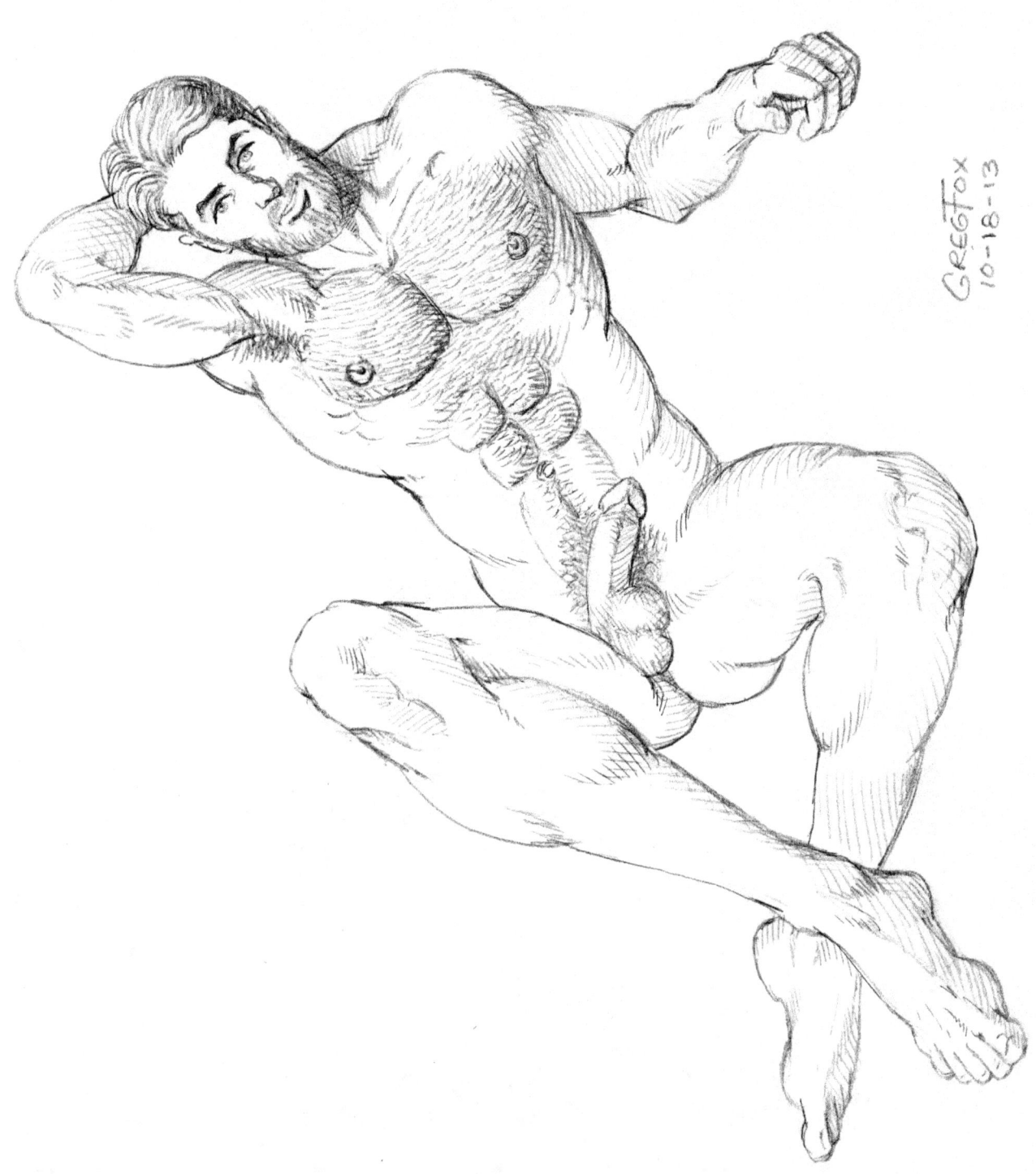

GregFox
10-18-13

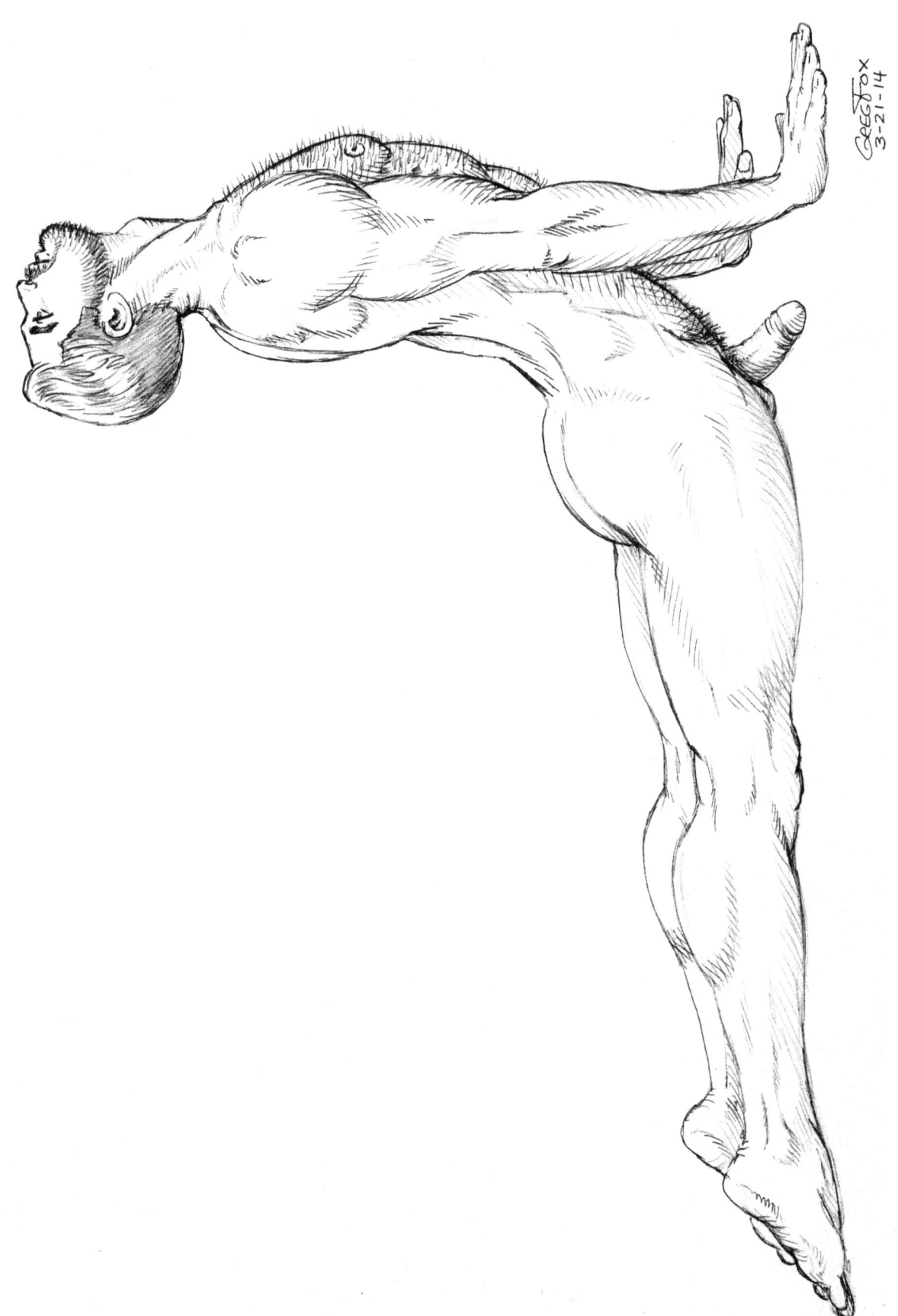

Hold on, we're not done yet! You were promised 50 drawings, and so far, you've seen 49. But now, for the 50th, you're going to get a chance to go behind the scenes and see how a drawing is done from the very beginning phases. Let's call this....

Anatomy of a Drawing

Phase 1: >>>
The first thing I do is a basic "stick figure", just to establish the stance and where the all the joints, (knees, wrists, shoulders, etc), are in relation to each other. This is the foundation on which the completed drawing will be built, so it's crucial here to get all those "establishing points" in the proper place.

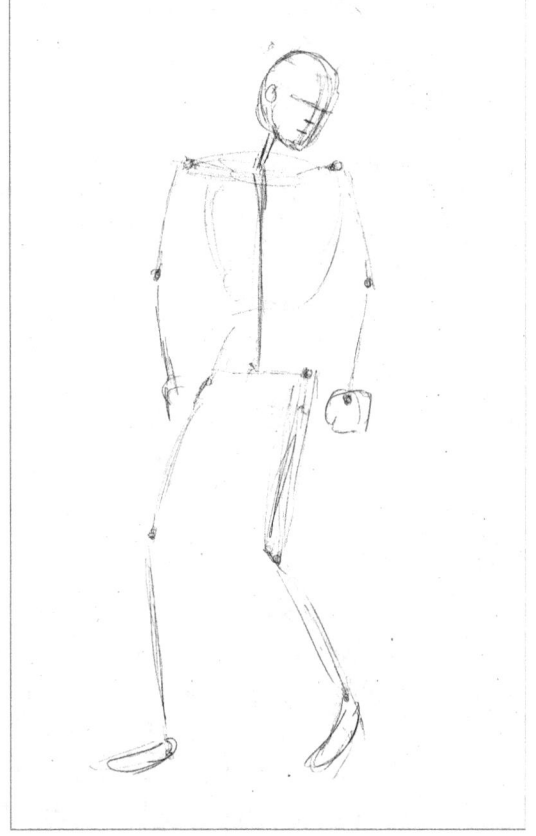

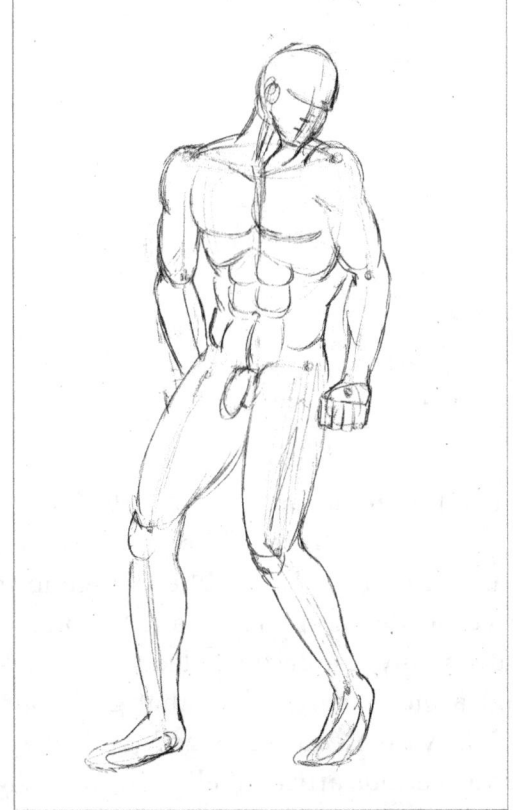

<<< Phase 2: Now I start to build the basic forms of the figure's surface and muscle structure. It's still loose and somewhat "sketchy", yet the basic forms of the muscles are there, anchored by the fact that the stick figure drawing in the previous phase, (which you can still see within this drawing), is assuring that everything is in the proper place.

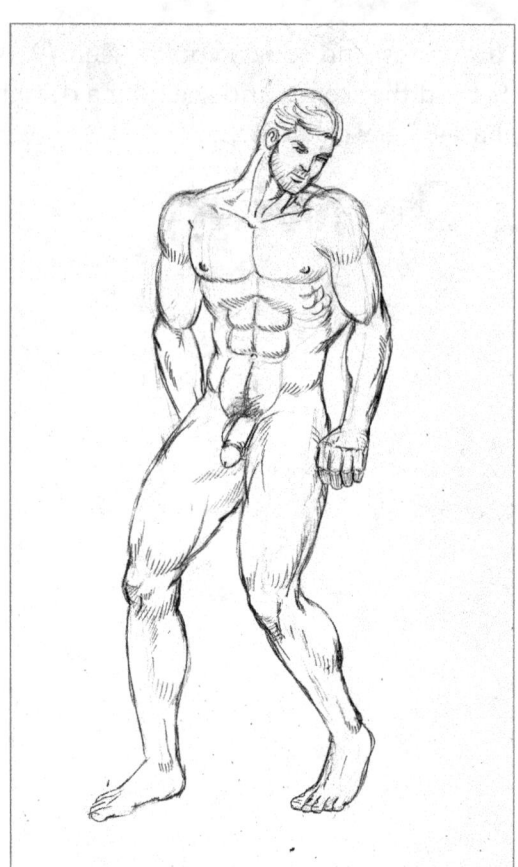

<<< Phase 3: In this phase, the surface structure of the figure gets rendered more realistically. The various muscles become more defined and areas of shading begin to emerge. The details of the feet and toes are delineated. Also, the face and hair are drawn in, (although still not as polished as they will ultimately look).

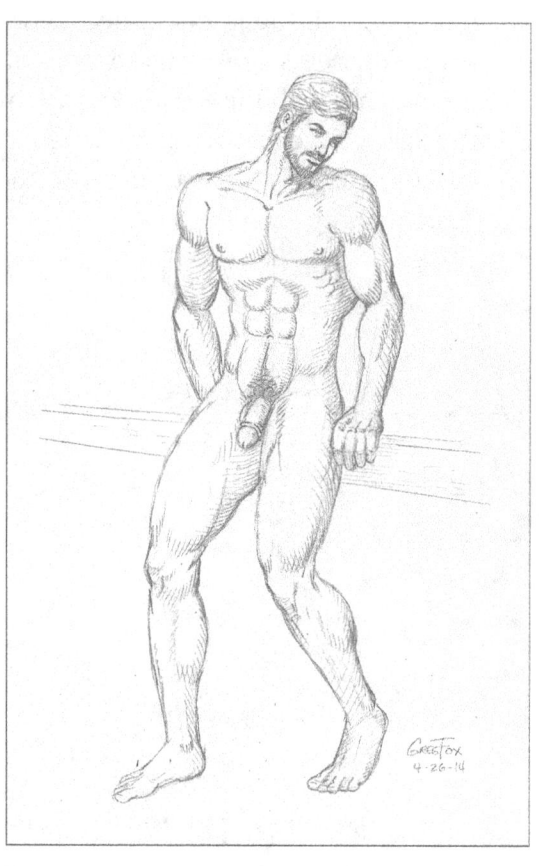

Phase 4: >>>

We're almost there, (but not quite). Now the various muscle structures are well defined; the shading has become much more intricate. The details of the hair and face have been delineated. All that's left is to add Drew's chest hair, right?

Phase 5: (On following page) >>>

Okay, so we weren't *quite* done in Phase 4. I'd been wanting to do something sort of "1920s-ish" for Drew, and this seemed like a good time to try it out. But the addition of the cap and socks, (and chest hair), aren't the only changes in the figure. I made a subtle change in the pectoral muscles, (they needed to be expanded a bit vertically), and I also made the biceps a bit less rounded off and more realistic looking. Additionally, the face needed a little more reworking, and the right elbow needed to be raised a bit. Finally, about that golf course background. It just seemed right! And that "Proper Golf Attire Required" sign? Well, okay... I do love that this book has given me a chance to be all "serious artist" n' all, but... that sign just shows a bit of the wiseass cartoonist shining through!

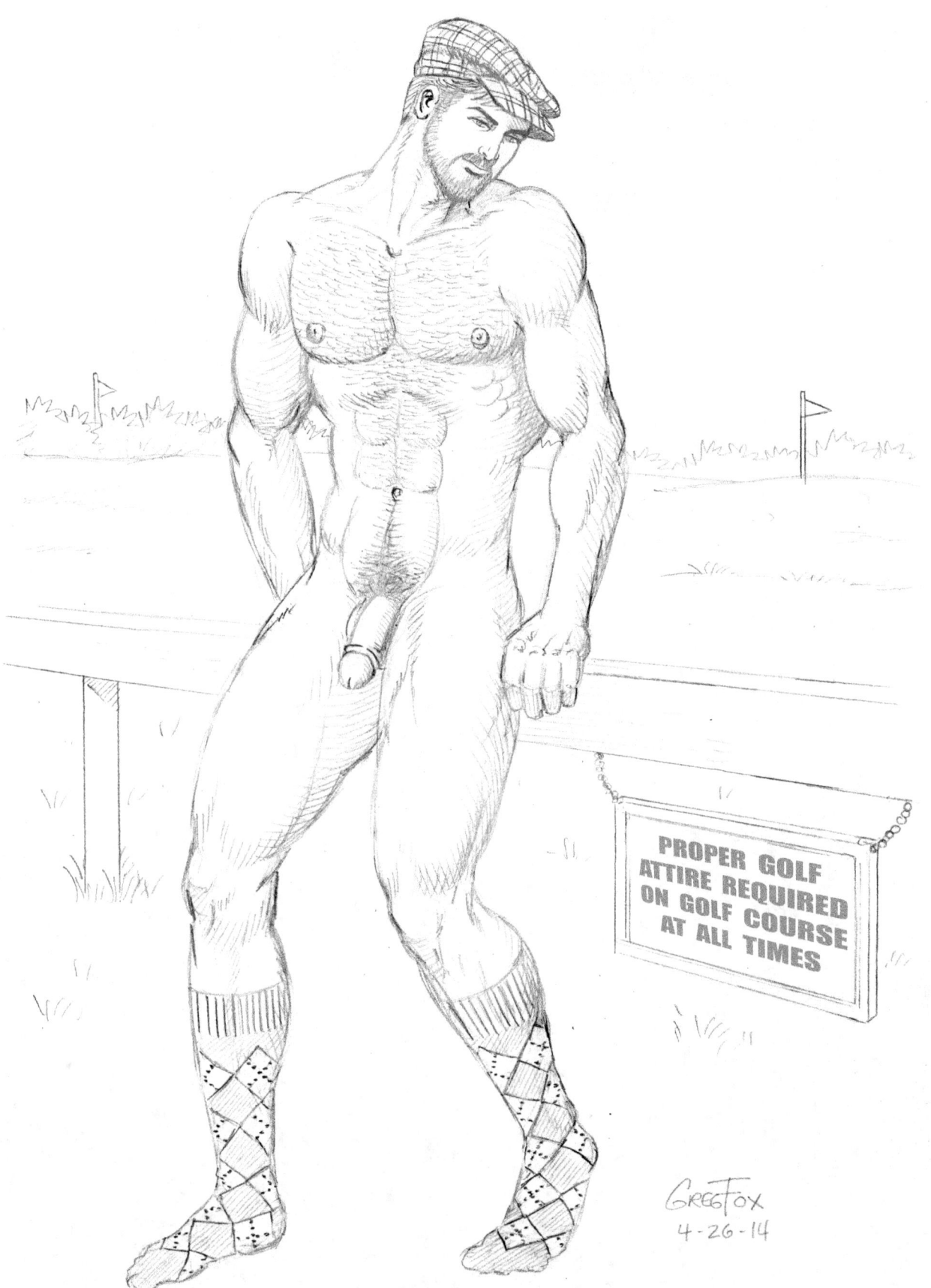

PROPER GOLF
ATTIRE REQUIRED
ON GOLF COURSE
AT ALL TIMES

GregFox
4-26-14

A Message From Drew Danvers

(As told to Greg Fox)

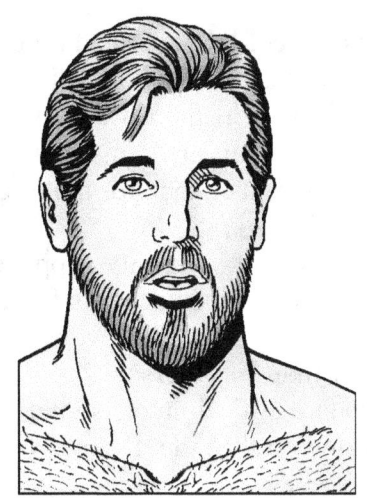

I ain't never posed naked for nothing before. Lotta folks may wonder how a good Christian boy from Alabama ended up dropping his drawers for these pictures, but... truth is, it wasn't no big deal.

I'd just graduated from University of Alabama in Huntsville, and was about to start the two-year master's degree program to become a licensed social worker. (Yeah, I may talk like a redneck... hell, I *am* a redneck. But that don't mean I ain't educated). It was a kinda strange time for me; most of my friends had now graduated, n' were off to start their careers, but here I was, hanging around campus for another two years to get my master's degree.

N' then I saw it. A flyer in the student union, about some students working on some kinda art project. A book of poetry they were putting together that they needed a "fit male model" for.

Well, I don't know a damn thing about poetry, but I was "fit", and I was "male", n' I figured I could take a stab at the "model" part.

Turns out, they were looking to sorta spice up this student poetry collection they were gonna publish at the end of the coming school year. 'Cause they lost a lotta money on the last one they published, not being able to sell nearly half the copies they printed.

So the idea was... get some campus jock to pose nude for some pictures, n' then include those pictures in the pages n' on the cover of the poetry collection. Maybe *that* might spark some sales.

Now, it sounds awful cold n' calculated the way I'm telling it. But the truth is, it wasn't that way at all. I liked these folks the second I met 'em. I'd spent the last four years at college hanging out with my fraternity buddies n' the guys on my football team, (no, UA Huntsville ain't got no official football team. That's UA Tuscaloosa. But we had our own "unofficial" touch football team that wasn't half as serious but probably twice as fun!). Anyways, these guys putting together the poetry book were real different from any of the folks on campus I was friends with. A real "artsy" kinda crowd, ya might say. But they were warm n' friendly, n' funny n' interesting. Hanging out with them, a lotta things started to become clear about myself that I'd been denying for a while, (but I guess that's a whole 'nother story).

Okay, back to the part about me posing nude, which is probably why you're reading this in the first place! I'd never had much experience in the "art world". My extra-curricular activities up to that point had been, like I said, playing football n' attending fraternity keg parties, (my friends used to say if there was a degree in "fraternity", I coulda had a double major). But I always had an interest in art. I just never felt confident, or competent, to *do* anything "artistic". But now, here, was a chance for me to get involved. So I said, "what the heck, let's do this".

The project was only supposed to take 2 or 3 weeks; it actually ended up lasting for about *8 months*! Which accounts for a coupla things: #1, I put on a little more muscle mass as time went on, (I was starting to work out more regularly that year), so you'll notice in some pics I'm more lean than in others. #2: My haircut is kinda different at various points along the way. Sometimes a little longer, sometimes a little shorter... sometimes parted in the middle, sometimes parted on the side. I've always liked to change it up; still do to this day. Why not, right?

One big change for me during that time was facial hair; I'd been mostly clean-shaven for my under-grad years. Some folks thought I grew the beard so I wouldn't get recognized in the nude pictures, but that ain't the case at all. I'd made the decision to grow a beard when I graduated with my bachelor's degree. I wanted to start the master's degree program with a new look, maybe something a little more mature. Or heck, maybe I just got tired of shaving! Anyways, I'm still rockin' the beard, so it sure wasn't no grad school phase. But who knows, maybe I'll shave it off tomorrow. Like I said, I like to change things up.

By the way, when the poetry book was finally published, it *sold out* of its initial printing! N' from what I understand, a number of copies were purchased by a whole bunch of my frat buddies! Yeah... I'm sure they were buying it just for the poems. Ha!

Was I at all concerned about posing nude? Not really. As far as any "controversy", well... there's a whole lotta male nudes throughout the history of art. Heck, Michelangelo's stuff is in a bunch of churches over in Italy, and ain't nobody can point at that n' say it's "scandalous" or whatever. And about me being nervous about taking off my clothes? By that point, I was pretty comfortable with my body. I'd had a few years of pudginess as a kid, but the years I'd spent working in my parents' peach orchard, (yeah, that's where the "Dixie Peach" tattoo comes from. Georgia may have lotsa peaches, but so does Alabama!), n' 'the years I'd spent playing touch football had gotten me into pretty good shape.

N' hey, even if I *wasn't* in so-called "good shape", I'd still like to think I woulda been okay with posing for those pictures. Personally, I think there's way too much emphasis in this culture on folks having "perfect" bodies, (whatever the heck *that* is). Trust me, in my work as a social worker, I seen an awful lotta folks punishing themselves 'cause they don't "measure up". Measure up? To *what*?

Now I ain't saying there's anything wrong with looking good... or with taking care of yourself, n' staying in good shape. I *do* think that's a *good* idea. But, the problem is, some folks are putting the cart before the horse, so to speak. The "body stuff" is *all* they care about. When really, that's only *one* ingredient in being a healthy, well-rounded person. What about character? What about doing good, meaningful work? What about contributing to society, n' making this planet a better place to live?

Folks who focus everything on the *body*, well... it's like baking a peach pie, n' all you focus on is the *crust*. You leave out the peaches n' all the other good stuff that goes inside, n' you just bake an empty pie crust. Who the heck wants *that*? I want *peaches* in *my* peach pie!

If seeing my body in the pictures in this here book inspires ya to get in shape, well... I s'pose that's a good thing. (Long as you do it *healthily*. N' don't even *dream* about using steroids or any other garbage. That's just plain *nuts*).

But I'd be even happier if you were inspired by the kinda *man* I am. The kinda guy who tries his best to do the right thing... who tries to help out folks less fortunate than himself... n' who cares about making this here world a better place, (trust me.... there are lotsa folks out there who need a hand... who are suffering n' in pain... or who just need a *friend*).

I say, focus on being healthy... and on being a good person. If you can go to bed at night knowing you did good work in the world... that you're making a positive difference here... that the world's a better place 'cause *you're* in it... then I got news for ya, my friend.

You're beautiful.

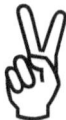

Drew

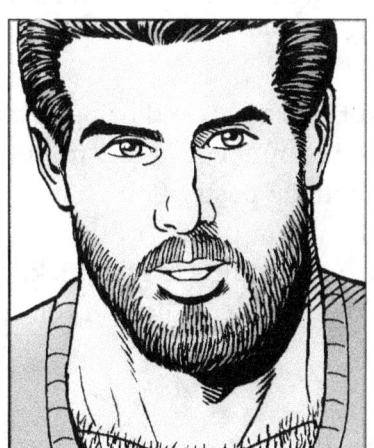

Drew's Peach Pie Recipe

"What I like about this recipe is that it combines the best of the South with a little touch of sweetness outta' the North. Livin' at Kyle's B&B, my good friend Kyle has kinda' inspired me to start eatin' real healthy, (not that I was ever a junk food junkie before. I mean… c'mon). For example, Kyle *never* uses plain ol' white sugar, or even "brown sugar". He likes to use maple syrup as a sweetener, (the real kind… not that cheap-o stuff that's got about 1% real maple in it). The good thing is, not only is it healthier… it also tastes *great*! He also doesn't use refined flours,… it's whole-grain flours all the way. And organic produce, too. This stuff is all easy to find in most big grocery stores, so… have fun with it. And save a slice for me!"

——Drew Danvers

PIE FILLING

INGREDIENTS:

- 4 cups sliced fresh peaches, approximately 2 lbs. (peeled or unpeeled, that's up to you. Mama always made it with unpeeled when I was growing up, and that's how Kyle makes it, too. Whatever ya' do, don't ya' dare use no *canned* peaches!).
- 3 tablespoons spring water
- ¼ teaspoon sea salt, (optional)
- 1 - 2 tablespoons whole wheat pastry flour (it's important to get pastry flour; plain old whole wheat flour won't be as fluffy when baked).
- 3 tablespoons of REAL maple syrup

1. Put the peaches, water, and salt into a pan and bring to a boil.
2. Turn down heat, cover, and let it simmer for a few minutes, (3 at most).
3. Mix in the maple syrup, and then the pastry flour.
4. Stir it real well, so it doesn't get all lumpy.
5. Cook for a few more minutes, until it starts to feel thick.
6. Turn off heat, and let it cool down some, while you start making your pie crust. (see next page)

PIE CRUST

- 3 cups whole wheat pastry flour
- ¼ teaspoon sea salt, (optional)
- ½ cup oil, (your choice of oil; Kyle usually uses coconut oil)
- ½ cup spring water

1. Mix together flour & salt in a big bowl.
2. Then stir in the oil as best you can using a fork, (it'll coat the flour till it kind of balls up).
3. Then add the water, stir in with a fork.
4. Using your hands, form the dough into one big ball.
5. Then take that and halve it into 2 equal-sized pieces.
6. Using a rolling pin on a lightly floured surface, roll out one half of the dough until it's flat and even, (some people put the dough between 2 sheets of wax paper when they do this, and peel off the wax paper when it's flattened).
7. Flip over the dough, and press it into your pie plate. Press around the edges to flatten it in the plate well. Using a fork, make some pricks around the dough.
8. Now, put it into a pre-heated 375 degree oven for approximately 10 minutes.
9. While that's baking, take the other half of that ball of dough, (that's going to be the top of your pie crust), and roll it out the same way you did the bottom half, and then put it off to the side.
10. Once the bottom half has baked for 10 minutes, remove from oven and scoop in the Pie Filling you made, (which should be cooled down a bit now).
11. Spread it out evenly within the pie crust, and cover with the top crust. Seal the edges by pinching with your fingers, and then poke some holes on top with a fork.
12. Bake in a pre-heated 375 degree oven for about 35—40 minutes. Check on it; you'll want the top surface to look golden brown.

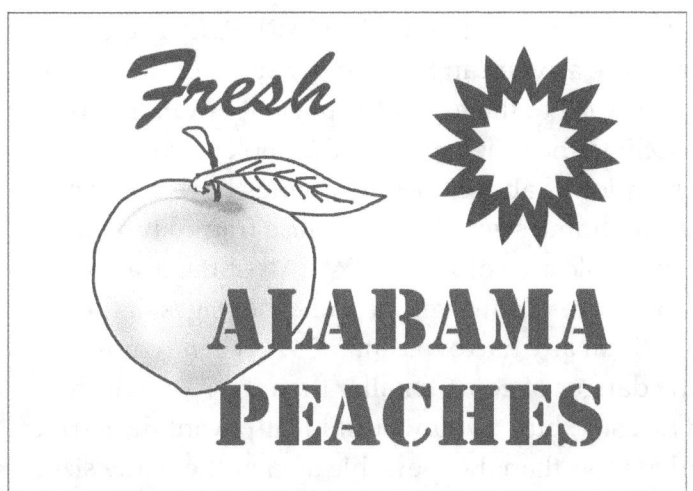

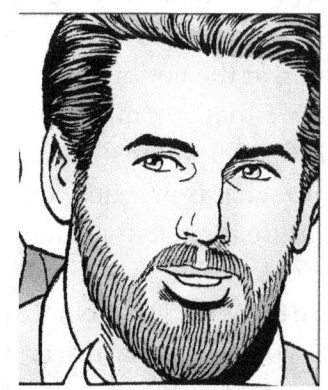

PAGE REMOVAL and FRAMING SUGGESTIONS:

What you'll need:
- A sharp cutting tool, such as an X-acto knife, box cutter, or even a fresh razor blade.
- A thin, solid surface to place behind the drawing you're going to remove from the book. It must be longer than 10 inches, (oh, stop it! That's the height of the book). A thin metal ruler would be ideal. If you don't have that, a thin manila folder will do.
- Some low-resistance tape, like artist's tape, drafting tape, of painter's tape, to lightly hold the pin-up in place when you are framing it.
- A frame with which to frame your print! My advice... if you happen to have a **Michael's** arts & crafts store in your area, they have a wonderful selection of frames, at very afford-able prices, (which often go on sale... it may pay to check their sale flyer for several weeks before buying. I've often bought frames there at 50% off!). The frame size you'll need is to hold 8" x 10" pictures; the kind that have a matte inside, which actually allows for a slightly smaller viewing area of 7 and 3/8" x 9 and 3/8". This is a very standard frame size, probably the most common size you'll find in stores, (and conveniently, the right size for ALL of the pin-ups in this book!).

Now follow these directions:

1. Place the book on your lap, and open it to the page of the drawing you want to remove from the book.
2. Now, turn the page one page ahead, and place your thin solid surface, (the metal ruler or manila folder), on that page.
3. Push the metal ruler/manila folder as far into the inner spine of the book as you can, and hold it there in place.
4. Turn back to the page of the drawing you want to remove, so that the drawing is now fac-ing you on your lap, and the metal ruler/manila folder is directly behind it, pressed into the inner spine of the book.
5. Now, with the book held open as WIDE as you can manage, VERY CAREFULLY, take your sharp cutting tool, and, (placing it as close as you can to the inner spine of the book), beginning at the bottom of the page, slice upward to the top of the page. It is VERY IM-PORTANT that you make the slice as CLOSE to the inner spine of the book as you can. (Why is this important? Here's why. As mentioned above, these drawings have been sized to fit into what is probably the most common frame size, 8" x 10". Those frames have a matte inside them that actually allows a viewable area of 7 3/8" x 9 3/8". All of the drawings in this book will fit into that 7 3/8" x 9 3/8" sized area. However, because the pages of the book are 8" wide, you do not want to slice them any narrower than 7 1/2" when removing them. If you go any narrower, you run the danger of going smaller than the 7 3/8" width of the matte's viewable size, which is not a disaster, but....you would ideally want the surface of the picture you're framing to be slightly larger than the viewable area of the matte size).
6. Once you've removed the drawing from the book...take a deep breath. You did it!

7. Now it's time to prepare the frame. Open up the frame so that you can take out the cardboard matte part.

8. On a clean table surface, , first place down the drawing you just removed from the book, (facing up), and then the cardboard matte from the frame over it. Play around a little with it to position the drawing within the matte so it looks centered.

9. This part is a little tricky. You need to flip over the cardboard matte and the drawing so the front of each are now facing down on the table, (while keeping the drawing in place where you had centered it in Step # 8).

10. You're now going to use 2 small slices of that artist's tape/painter's tape to lightly secure the drawing to the matte. One piece of tape on 2 of the drawing's corners, diagonally opposed, will work. You want to make sure the drawing is in the proper position in the matte which, I know, is hard to do now that it's facing downward. Just try it a few times til you get it right, (that's why you're using the low-sticky artist/painter's type tape). If you happen to own a light-box, this will make things much easier... you can place the matte and drawing on the light-box, and see through the drawing to make sure it's centered properly before taping it.

11. Once the drawing is correctly taped to the cardboard matte, you can easily pop it into the frame, close it up, and ta-da... it's ready to be hung! Nice work! That wasn't so hard, was it?

Here's an open invitation: if you frame & hang any of the drawings in this book, snap a pic of it, showing how it looks in your house or apartment, (you can be in the pic, too!). With your permission, I'll post those pics on the Kyle's B&B website and **Facebook** page.
Just send to: KylesBnB@aol.com
Or, if you're on **Facebook**, post to the Kyle's B&B **Facebook** page at
www.facebook.com/kylecomics

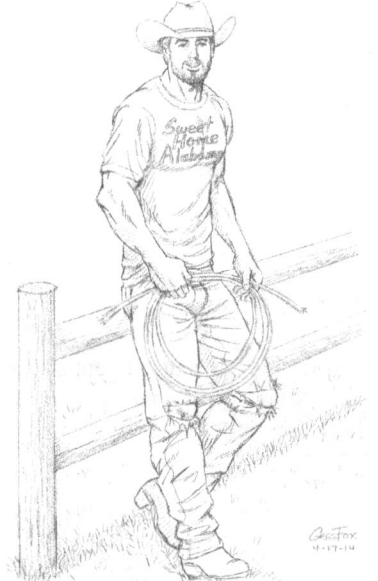

ABOUT THE ARTWORK

The majority of the drawings were done on 8½" x 11" bristol board, and have been reproduced here at close to or at their original size. Five of them were done on tinted 12" x 18" charcoal paper and have been reduced more significantly to fit the parameters of this book.

As of this writing, (May, 2014), as the book is going to print, I have already received some inquiries about the availability of the original art for purchase. Most of the pieces are available; if there is a particular piece you're interested in, feel free to contact me at KylesBnB@aol.com

---

ACKNOWLEGEMENTS

There are so many to thank for helping this book come to be. Starting with

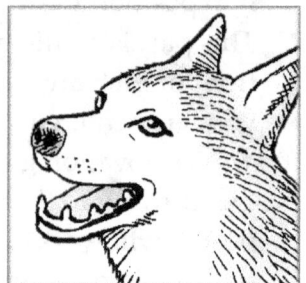

- My mother, whose character, humor, and love continue to echo through every panel of **Kyle's B&B**. I miss you every day!

- The rest of my family, in New York, California, and beyond. Thank you for your love and belief in me.

- Richard, Julie, Bobby Klein and everyone at **Book Revue** bookstore in Huntington, Long Island, NY. My "second home" for so many years!

- My friends far and wide… from Huntington, Geneseo, Spize, Sam Ash, Northport, Book Revue, the Berndt Toast gang, and elsewhere. Thank you for lifting me up and making me smile!

- The town of Northport, Long Island, NY.

- For the many models who have been kind enough to pose for me over the years, in art classes and in various drawing groups. Thank you for your strength, your creativity, and the inspiration you have brought!

- The many newspapers and magazines who have published **Kyle's B&B** over the years. Thank you for your support of my work! Some, sadly, no longer with us, such as the **Chicago Free Press**, New England's **In Newsweekly**, **Outlook-Long Island**, and the **Orange County-Long Beach Blade** of southern California. Others, thankfully, still going strong, like the **Philadelphia Gay News**, **Out in Jersey**, Rochester's **The Empty Closet, David-Atlanta, Q-Salt Lake**, Iowa's **AccessLine,** the **Gayzette** of Omaha, Nebraska, **Liberty Press** of Kansas, and **What's Happening Magazine** of Florida!

- **Bent-Con** and all of the wonderful people I have been honored to meet there!

- The Long Island Gay & Lesbian Film Festival

- **Prism Comics,** for being a strong voice for LGBT comics!

- Kathy O'Marra, for being such a strong supporter of my work all these years. *And* for being a great friend!

- Joe Giella

- My friend Grant, for his Vermont hospitality and fun conversations!

- Misty, Ginger, and Midnight

- Marianne Williamson, for your inspiration and for being a sparkling light in this world.

- The readers of **Kyle's B&B**, who make this all such a joy. Thank you for your magnificent support, interest, comments, letters, e-mails, Facebook comments, (and "likes"!), gifts, and expressions of love. And of course, for buying my books! I am just overwhelmed with gratitude for how you have taken this comic strip, its characters and stories, into your hearts. Thank you SO MUCH!!!!!

- The Angels, St. Jude, Jesus Christ, and the Holy Spirit.

- And of course, God, for all of the love, light, and joy. And for so many miracles along the way!

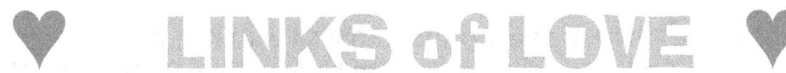

I'd be remiss if I didn't take a moment to point out some websites of organizations that, from what I can tell, and as of this date, are doing major-league amazing work to help bring some light into this world. If you have the time and inclination, I encourage you to visit some of their websites and find out more about them for yourself.

www.doctorswithoutborders.org   **Doctors Without Borders**, (Médecins Sans Frontières), Providing emergency medical care around the world in desperate situations.

www.oxfamamerica.org   **Oxfam** is an international confederation of 15 organizations working in more than 90 countries worldwide to find lasting solutions to poverty and related injustice around Providing emergency medical care around the world in desperate situations.

www.glwd.org   **God's Love We Deliver** is the tri-state area's, (NY, NJ, CT). leading provider of nutritious, individually-tailored meals to people who are too sick to shop or cook for themselves.

www.angelfood.org   **Project Angel Food** Providing daily meals for people homebound or disabled by HIV/AIDS and other serious illnesses in Los Angeles.

www.TheHungerSite.com (Click & Donate Free Food!)

www.world.org   A spectacular directory of links to websites dedicated to the environment & holistic health

www.FreeRice.com (Play game & Donate Free Rice!)

www.iglhrc.org   (the International Gay & Lesbian Human Rights Campaign)

www.jflag.org   J-FLAG's mission is to work towards a Jamaican society in which the Human Rights and Equality of Lesbians, All-Sexuals, and Gays are guaranteed.

www.gmhc.org   **The Gay Men's Health Crisis** (GMHC) is a NYC-based non-profit, volunteer-supported and community-based AIDS service organization that has led the United States in the fight against AIDS.

www.whyhunger.org   **Why Hunger** (formerly World Hunger Year). Working to eradicate world hunger.

www.TheTrevorProject.org   Focused on suicide prevention efforts among LGBTQ youth

www.thursdayschildofli.org   A non-profit agency providing support & housing for people with hiv/aids on Long Island.

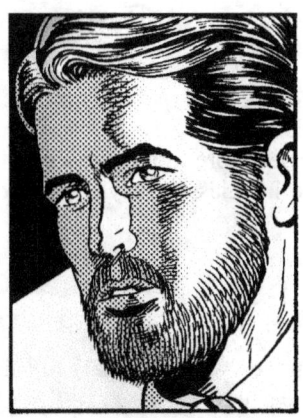

www.Care2.com (Click on Take Action/Petition Site)

www.VolunteerMatch.org

www.marrow.org   (Save a life/Donate bone marrow)

www.stjude.org   St. Jude's Children's Hospital

www.One.org

www.Water.org

www.Kiva.org

Want to see more of Drew? You can visit with him anytime, and catch up with him and his friends at **Kyle's Bed & Breakfast!**

*Your local LGBT publication **doesn't** carry **Kyle's B&B** ? Be sure to visit the **Kyle's B&B WEBSITE** to see new episodes as they are posted, (new episode every other Tuesday!).*

WWW.KYLECOMICS.COM

(and while you're at it, let that local paper of yours know that you want Kyle's B&B running in there!)

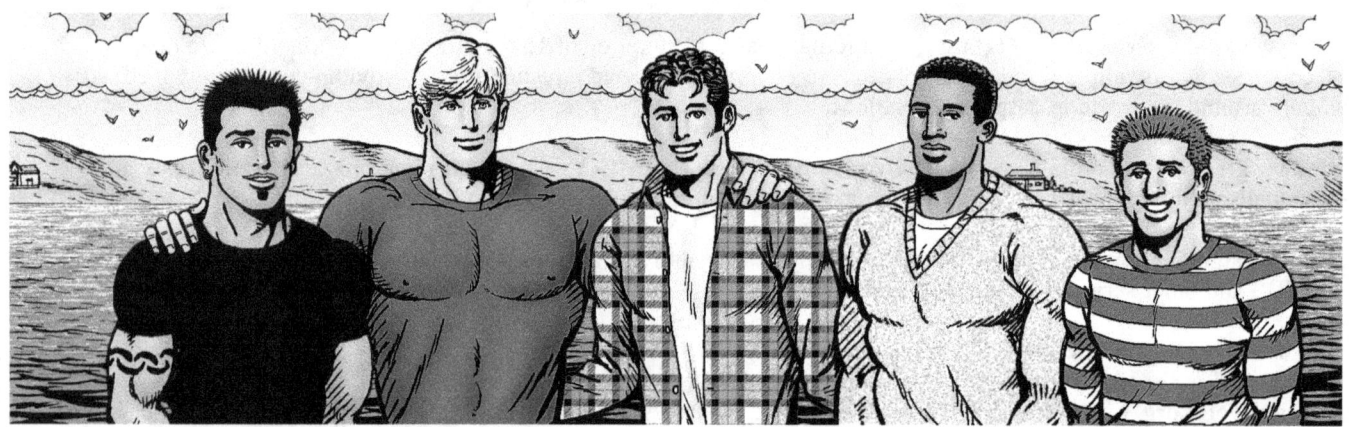

Also, stay connected with the B&B through

FACEBOOK

www.facebook.com/kylecomics

is the official Kyle's B&B fan page
on Facebook!!!

Click "LIKE" when you're there, and you'll be kept updated when new episodes are posted, get new book release info as it happens, *and* get all sorts of other B&B tidbits to tide you over between episodes!

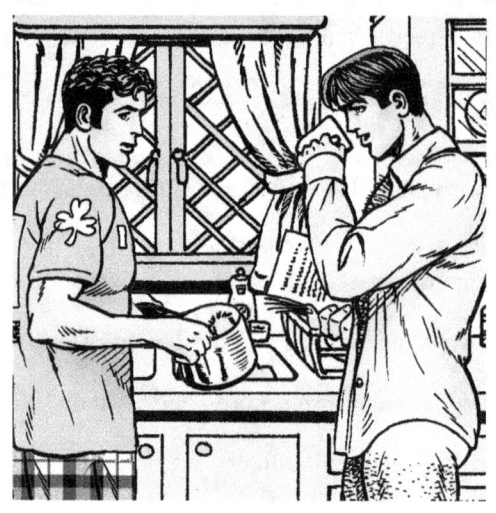

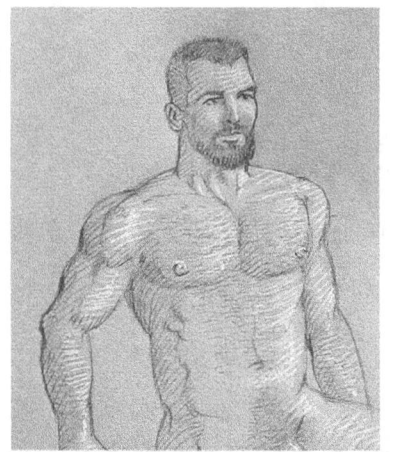

The Figure Drawings of Greg Fox

From his days at Geneseo College up to the present, Greg Fox has studied classical figure drawing. Though a bit different than his comics work, it's very clear to see how one influences the other. If you'd like to see more of this artwork, he has a separate website that's dedicated specifically to his classical style figure drawings. Some of which is for sale. The address is:

www.gregfox.net

Please note… this website contains plenty of images with (tasteful) full-frontal male nudity. Therefore, it is only for those over the age of 18.

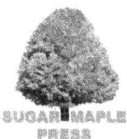
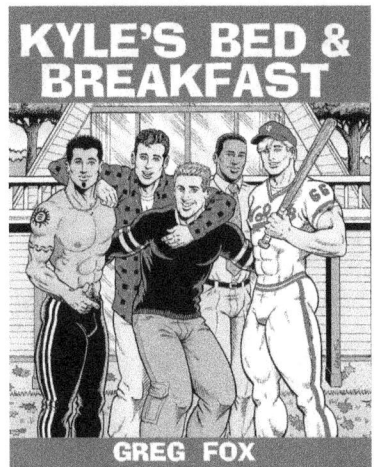
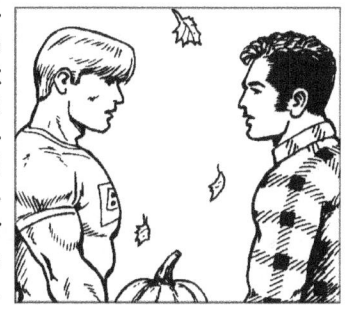
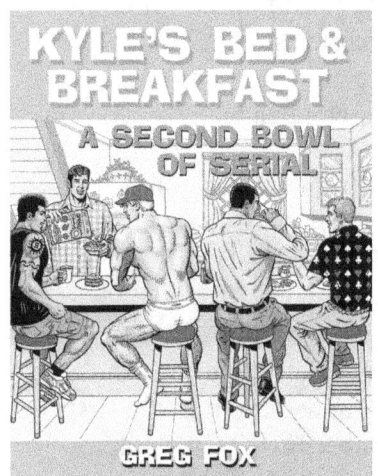
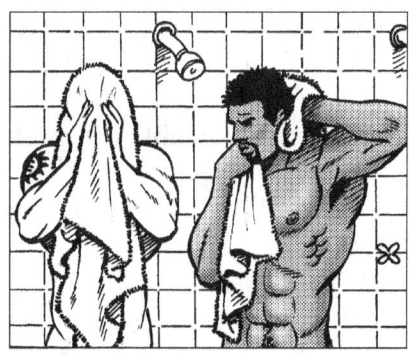
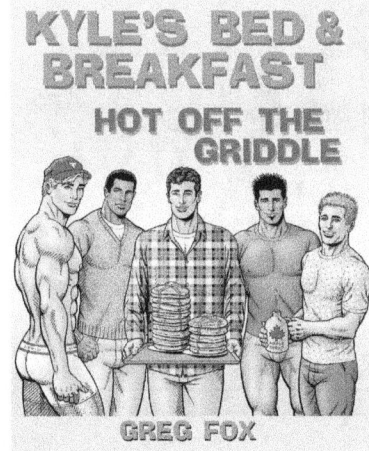
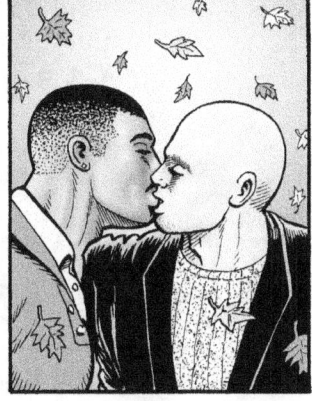

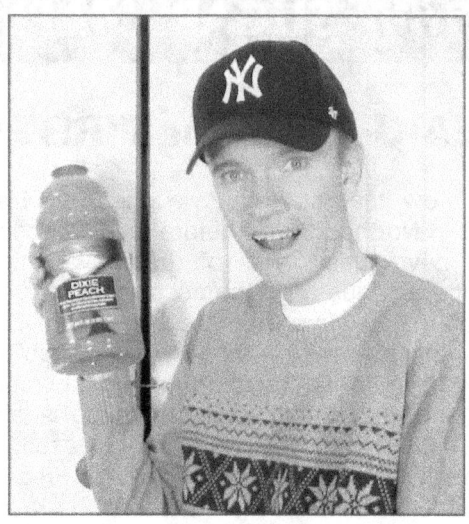

Greg Fox began making comics at 12 years old, publishing his first strip at age 14 in his high school newspaper and continuing to illustrate and write comic strips through high school and college. He received a B.A. from Geneseo College in upstate New York. Immediately following college, he played guitar in several New York-based rock bands, but then jumped into doing comics full-force. His illustration work has appeared in comic books for a number of companies, including Triumphant Comics, and Marvel Comics, and in magazines such as Blue, the Advocate, Genre, and many others. He is also the writer/artist for such comic strips as "**Manic Music**", (based on his experience in the rock music world), and "**An Angel's Story**".

Fox's most notable comic strip, "**Kyle's Bed & Breakfast**", premiered in late 1998. The strip is currently syndicated to a variety of publications across North America, and also has a worldwide following on the web. Fox published the first book collection of **Kyle's B&B** in September, 2004. The book was a Lambda Literary Award Finalist for "Best Humor Book" of the year in 2005. He was the grand-prize winner of the "Life Without Fair Courts" cartoon contest in 2007, sponsored by Lambda Legal. A second collection of Kyle's B&B, "**Kyle's Bed & Breakfast: A Second Bowl of Serial**" was published in April, 2012. A new edition of the first volume of Kyle's B&B was published by Sugar Maple Press in November, 2012. In September, 2013, a third collection of Kyle's B&B was published, "**Kyle's Bed & Breakfast: Hot Off the Griddle**", marking the strip's debut in full color. **The Sugar Maple Press Anthology of Nature Poems,** published in Spring of 2014, featured Greg Fox as editor and photographer.

Fox currently resides in Northport, Long Island, New York, busily working on new episodes of Kyle's B&B, and several other book projects for Sugar Maple Press, as well as the fourth volume of the **Kyle's Bed & Breakfast** series. He can be reached at: KylesBnB@aol.com

His work can be seen at www.kylecomics.com

Thank You!

www.ingramcontent.com/pod-product-compliance
Lightning Source LLC
Chambersburg PA
CBHW081002170526
45158CB00010B/2877